W9-ANI-484

AND TYLER TOO

Also by Donald Barr Chidsey

Andrew Jackson, Hero

The Day They Sank the *Lusitania*

Elizabeth I: A Great Life in Brief

The French and Indian War

The Great Conspiracy: Aaron Burr and His Strange Doings in the West

The Great Separation: The Story of the Boston Tea Party and the Beginning of the American Revolution

July 4, 1776

Lewis and Clark: The Great Adventure

The Louisiana Purchase

The Loyalists: The Story of Those Americans Who Fought Against Independence

Mr. Hamilton and Mr. Jefferson

On and Off the Wagon: A Sober Analysis of the Temperance Movement from the Pilgrims Through Prohibition

The Panama Canal

Shackleton's Voyage

Sir Walter Raleigh, That Damned Upstart

The Spanish-American War

The Tide Turns: An Informal History of the Campaign of 1776 in the American Revolution

Valley Forge

The War in the North

The War in the South

The War with Mexico

Wars in Barbary

The World of Samuel Adams

AND TYLER TOO

★ ★ ★

Donald Barr Chidsey

THOMAS NELSON INC., PUBLISHERS
Nashville New York

 Published in Nashville, Tennessee, by Thomas Nelson Inc., Publishers, and simultaneously in Don Mills, Ontario, by Thomas Nelson & Sons (Canada) Limited. Manufactured in the United States of America.

First edition

Library of Congress Cataloging in Publication Data

Chidsey, Donald Barr.
And Tyler too.

Bibliography: p.139
Includes index.
1. Tyler, John, Pres. U.S., 1790–1862.
2. Presidents—United States—Biography.
3. United States—Politics and government—1841-1845. I. Title.
E397.C47 973.5'8'0924 78-807
ISBN 0-8407-6585-1

Contents

AND TYLER TOO

1

★ ★ ★

The Millennium of the Minnows

The country had gone mad. East and west, north and south, it had been taken over by raving lunatics who screeched at every crossroads, while bands played furiously and marchers waved silly flags, chanting silly songs.

Eighteen-forty! The National Republicans—the Whigs, they were calling themselves now—circled their Democratic enemies, slavering. Eighteen-forty would tell the tale. It would usher in the Era of Hoopla. It would be the time when the screaming started.

The Whigs, proud of their new name, had high plans. They proposed to campaign for the Presidency with floats in the East, slangwhangers in the West. The South, they reckoned, could more or less take care of itself.

The masterminds of the party had decided that 1840 must be an anti campaign rather than a pro—that is, folks out there should not be urged to vote *for* "our" candidate but rather *against* "theirs." "Their" candidate would unquestionably be the incumbent President, a fussy little dude named Martin Van Buren. "Ours," it was assumed by the unknowing, would be Henry Clay.

Clay—the Mill Boy of the Slashes, Harry of the West, the Great Pacificator, son of a Baptist minister, who liked to play brag for high stakes and usually won, whose capacity for Monongahela whiskey was famous—Clay *was* the Whig party.

He had virtually created it single-handed. Since 1812—he had been one of the War Hawks who brought about that unfortunate conflict—he had been weaning wealthy dissidents away from the Jeffersonian Democrats, and now he seemed supreme in his own set. The American System was his. He was its spokesman, as he had been its author. He shone alone in that somewhat murky empyrean, and not a millionaire in the land but was willing to pay him tribute. He stood for a high selective tariff, a central banking system in private hands, federal assistance for the states in the building of roads and canals, a strong Presidency. Also, he was a famous orator.

This period in American history is called the Millennium of the Minnows, presumably because the little fish that flipped and flopped around in the Congressional tank all thought they were whales.* It was the time of the three-hour Senatorial speech, when oratory was judged by eloquence, yes, but judged even more critically by

*Theodore Roosevelt, a famous phrase maker, used this term in his biography of Thomas Hart Benton, and he has sometimes been credited with its invention, but examples have been found in journals much earlier, and Parton (*Jackson,* III, 179) calls "millennium of the minnows" a "common remark of the time."

sheer weight, poundage, like a bagged elephant. Even the demigods—Haynes, Benton, Webster—emitted only words, howsoever ponderous. Like Burke in England, like the elder Pitt, they raised rhapsodic applause but changed no vote. Henry Clay could be considered in this class, a hurler of thunderbolts that were not expected to hit anything and wouldn't have harmed it if they had. As one Senator, Augustus H. Shepperd of North Carolina, put it, rather pettishly: "Clay could get more men to run after him to hear him speak, but fewer to vote for him, than any man in America."

So in 1840 it was decided by the Whig leaders in convention assembled at Harrisburg, Pennsylvania—by no means all of the delegates or even a majority of them—that Harry of the West should be passed over. By means of the so-called unit rule of voting, introduced here for the first time in American politics—for this was the first rigged convention†—they contrived to nominate instead an ambitious nonentity from Ohio, William Henry Harrison.

Clay himself did not attend the convention. When, back in Kentucky, he heard what had happened (admittedly he'd been drinking at the time) he flew into a rage. He slambanged back and forth, shouting that his friends weren't worth the powder to blow them to hell. But he quieted down when he saw what was being done without him, and he worked hard in the campaign. Clay was a good party man.

†But not the first political convention. That had been convened at Philadelphia, September 11, 1836, by the Anti-Mason Party, which established several important precedents, including the issuance of a party platform, called then a "statement of principles." Since all the men the party really wanted to nominate were high Masons, they fell back on a nobody named William Wirt. He lost.

What did Harrison stand for? Who knew? The chief things about him were his lack of enemies and the fact that he was, technically, a hero. He was a major general in the regular army, not just a militia officer, and although he had never been involved in any momentous military operation, his two brushes with the Indians—Tippecanoe and the Thames—were rated as victories; and that made him a hero, didn't it? His age was seldom mentioned. He was sixty-seven, older by far than any previous Presidential candidate. It was a time when well-liked generals often were given "Old" nicknames by their admiring men—"Old Hickory," "Old Fuss and Feathers," "Old Rough and Ready," as more lately they have been called "Old Iron Pants" and "Old Blood and Guts." William Henry Harrison's men, however, referred to him as "Granny," without flattering intent. In their eyes he was about ready for the grave.

His political record was scarcely impressive. A Virginian born, a member of the planter aristocracy, he had spent most of his life in the public service—secretary of the Northwest Territory, briefly a Congressman, governor of Indiana Territory, minister to Colombia. Though in his letter of acceptance of the nomination he described himself as "a retired and unpretending individual," he maintained a mansion at North Bend, Ohio, that was one of the sights of the rivers—steamboats slowed down there in order to give their passengers a chance to gasp at the grandeur of the place—and presently he was clerk of the common pleas court of Hamilton County, Ohio, a sinecure.

His public service, then, should be played down, his military service played up. Of the two battles he had commanded, neither glorious, that of the Thames, in

Canada, was the more notable. Not just Indians had been the enemy then but some British, even some British *regulars,* whereas at Tippecanoe Harrison had picked a bad position, allowed himself to be surprised, and lost many men, although eventually he swept the field. Still, "the Thames" was hard to say, especially when it was learned that in Canada, as in London, it was pronounced "Tems," which would sound silly to Americans, whereas "Tippecanoe" had a fine martial swing to it. So it was that the managers among the Whigs, those who had nominated William Henry Harrison at the party's first convention, now declared that the paragon should hereafter be known as Old Tippecanoe.

Besides, the slogan "Tippecanoe and Tyler Too" was irresistible. Who could lose with that lovely, alliterative war-cry?

When it came to selecting a Vice-Presidential nominee, the Whigs decided that this should be a man who stood for everything General Harrison didn't stand for. They commanded a coalition rather than a party, and they feared to lose great masses of converts if they made clear their essential beliefs. So, they surmounted this difficulty in a manner that was to become traditional in American politics. They picked John Tyler, an Easterner (Harrison was a Westerner), a defected Democrat, a comparatively young man, who was opposed to federal support for interstate communications—the opposite in every respect to William Henry Harrison.

This was called "balancing the ticket." It is still practiced by both parties, clearly on the assumption that all regular nominees for the Presidency are immortal.

The man thus honored was not taken by surprise. A gentleman is never surprised. John Tyler was tall, handsome, amiably if conventionally eloquent, a man who thought of himself as a tag-end of the Virginia Dynasty, a firm believer in everything Jeffersonian. What was he doing in the ranks of the Whigs? He believed that he had been disowned by his own party, the orthodox Democrats, and that he could best serve his country and the cause of states' rights by taking refuge in the enemy camp. He was conscientious about this. It was a point of honor with him. Tyler, an old-fashioned man, courteous, chivalrous, was as touchy about his honor as any newly adubbed twelfth-century knight. Also, he was ambitious, and though he knew that the Clayites welcomed him because they thought he might hold the South in that somehow shaky confederation—at least until it had jelled into a firm, meaningful party—he really seems to have believed that he could bring these bolters, these Whigs, around to the proper Jeffersonian way of thinking. He was, of course, mistaken.

Money was no object. This was at once apparent. Never before had the election of a President been thought of as an expense; never before had funds been accumulated for a campaign. No accounting was ever made—there were no laws to require such an accounting—but it was obvious from the beginning that a war chest had been raised, so that bands were hired, and wagons for floats, and horses, and fiery orators, with a free hand—at least among the Whigs. Many more were to vote in this election than ever had voted before—this was assumed—and many, many more were to take part in the vote-catching tricks to which the party resorted, all of them paid without hesitation or haggling. Not in vain did the new party number in its ranks the manufacturers, the bankers and brokers, and big-time planters. The backstage scenery movers at that Harrisburg convention, though they said nothing about this in public, clearly had reflected that as long as they had all those millionaires lined up, they might as well make some use of them.

A larger problem faced the masterminds at Harrisburg. Ever since the Anti-Masons launched the system in 1836 (see note page 11), the national convention had become a fixed part of American politics, an institution not to be altered or too much tampered with. This the professionals could endure, though they didn't pretend to like it. But the party platform loomed as a much larger snag in their stream of operations. It must be met in detail, each plank plainly presented, which could cause great pain to some of the contributors. The Whig machine was a monstrous thing, shivering and squealing with unspent energy, and it was held together with rubber bands and second-class paste, and would never stand up under pressure. How would the banking issue be met without infuriating either the East or the West, quite possibly both at the same time, or without seeming to favor Matty Van's middle course, the subtreasury plan? How could preferential tariff imposts be explained without recourse to that dreaded word "subsidies"? Who would hold those generous manufacturers in line for another campaign if a single plank of the platform-to-be seemed to frown upon protection, or the planters of the South if one didn't? Who would respect a "statement of principles" that made no mention of these burning issues?

It is the instinctive reaction of any politician, when faced with a dilemma such as this, to sidestep, to evade, to give forth semipromises that seem to relate to the matter at hand but really don't. But how can you slur over, how can you blur and obfuscate a whole national credo?

A child, glared at by such an ogre, might close his eyes and keep them closed as long as he could, in the hope that when he opened them again, the thing would be gone. The early Whigs were not children, but they came up with the same solution: Ignore the whole thing. If they kept their eyes closed forever, maybe the ogre really would go away.

The people, increasing numbers of whom were asking questions these days, had taken avidly to the custom of the party platform or statement of principles, which already had almost the force of law, and they would miss it, demanding something else in its place. This, too, the masterminds had anticipated. They and their hired orators and editors would not stand *for* anything, true. But they would stand *against* something—to wit: whatever the other side sought.

Out of this thinking there emerged, then, a great American political maxim: *If you have nothing to say, say it at the top of your lungs.*

This seems silly? It would be silly today. But it worked in 1840.

There had never been a Presidential election campaign like that of 1840; and we should pray to heaven that there will never be another.*

*"Probably at no other time in the history of our country have politicians been more successful in the use of language to obscure thought. . . . If it is true that the American people like to be humbugged, they had abundant reason to be pleased with the methods of this rollicking campaign." Chitwood, *John Tyler,* 183. "There has probably never been a presidential campaign of more enthusiasm and less thought." Schurz, *Henry Clay,* II, 186.

2

★ ★ ★

Here Come the Slangwhangers!

The man they called King of the Slangwhangers, Sergeant S. Prentiss, came from Mississippi, but he did not ply his trade in the Deep South during the horrendous campaign of 1840. Rather, he confined himself, as most of the others did, to what was later to be called the Middle West—Illinois, Michigan, Ohio, Indiana, sometimes Kentucky or Tennessee. He was fond of telling the audiences he harangued that "credit is the poor man's capital," which seemed to console them. He was short and had a gimp leg. He would windmill his arms, and his face would go red, as he gave 'em hell. He was usually drunk—sometimes very drunk—when they pushed him up on the platform, and so violent was his address that men soon were laying bets on how long he would last before collapsing. It was ordinarily at least three hours, often more.

There was Hugh Swinton Legaré of South Carolina. Scion of an established aristocratic family, when he slangwhanged through five states in 1840, he wore linsey-woolsey instead of his accustomed broadcloth and never was seen without a coonskin cap, though he quoted Latin from time to time just to prove that he was a scholar. Neither in Latin nor in English did he make any mention of America's problems or the Whigs' plans.

There was Senator William C. Preston, another South Carolinian, a great-nephew of Patrick Henry and quite as perfervid, if not as memorable, a speechmaker. It was to Senator Preston that Henry Clay wrote, a little later, that he would rather be right than be President, neglecting to mention that he wouldn't object to being both.

Undoubtedly the most distinguished of them all was The Archangel, Daniel Webster. He was the highest-priced constitutional lawyer in the country. A dark-haired, dark-complected fellow—Black Dan, they used to call him at Dartmouth—he had large censorious eyes that glowed in their cavernous, death's-head sockets. His very presence was a reproach to the poor mortal sinners he faced, but when he consented to speechify, men swooned, dogs flumped down upon their bellies, and birds, dazed, toppled right out of the trees. He could use words nobody understood, and it was generally conceded that all of his utterances were imperishable.

"Good heavens, he is a small cathedral by himself!" the Reverend Sydney Smith cried after meeting Webster.

A New Englander who hated Clay and who had his own eyes on the White House, Daniel Webster was an exception to the slangwhanger rule of route. But he traipsed over a good stretch of countryside in the northeast, meeting every appointment, to finish with a three-hour oration delivered in a cold rain at Francestown, New Hampshire, after which he was laid up for a week with flu. He was paid $63,000, a record, for the whole job.

The expressions "stump speaking" and "stumping" are known to have originated in the West at about this time, there being so many eminently mountable tree stumps scattered throughout a country only just retrieved from the wilderness. But the slangwhangers were no stump speakers. There was nothing inpromptu about their performances. Their engagements were made well in advance, their itineraries laid out, and their pay agreed upon. Elaborate platforms were built, sometimes bandstands as well—though never grandstands. The people who from miles around came on horseback or afoot, often in springless wagons, to the open meadow or hayfield in which the rally was to be staged didn't expect to be provided with seats unless there was a barbecue connected with the affair, in which case they took their turns. The speech itself, the main act, was always witnessed from a standing position, although it was guaranteed to last at least three hours without pause. It if rained, that was too bad. Chairs or stools, if there were any, were reserved for invalids, cripples, or Very Important Persons.

The slangwhangers of 1840 opened a whole new life to the scattered inhabitants of what was still regarded as the American frontier. Cities there, even towns, were few and far between. Opera or concerts were unknown, as were legitimate theater presentations, even Shakespeare. The minstrel show, soon to become a standby, as yet was rare. There were no circuses or carnivals and no strolling bands of acrobats. Those lucky enough to live near a river port or some landing place where the steamboats paused to pick up firewood were sometimes granted a sight of bits of grandeur—lace parasols, deep-piled carpeting, table silver, glass-prism chandeliers—but these were glimpses at best, and anyway there were hundreds of thousands of backswoodmen who never saw a steamboat from one year to the next. The camp meeting, the revival meeting, was known in the Ohio Valley and the South, where it was frowned upon by most plantation managers because it tended to stir up the slaves, but it had not yet penetrated Michigan and Wisconsin. The Whig slangwhangers met a real need of these lonely people, even though nobody could understand what they were screeching about, and ordinarily the eats and drinks were free.

"Slangwhanger" and "slangwhanging," as words, seem to have risen for the occasion of the campaign of 1840, which they did not long survive.* Thereafter, together with the verb "to slangwhang," they dropped out of the language.

There were of course lesser practitioners of this art, men every whit as loud and as long-winded, but of less exalted lineage, and untitled. These, too, were well paid, and when they had proved their drawing power heavily booked. Commonly they posed as workingmen, exhibiting for the skeptical some of the tools of their trade. This was in part to counteract any possible influence of the

*The *Oxford English Dictionary* defines "slangwhang" as "To assail with, to make use of, violent language, abuse, or vituperation," and "slangwhanger" as "A noisy or abusive talker or writer," and traces them back, somewhat unconvincingly, to 1829. The *Dictionary of American English* has it only as "Nonsense," and gives an 1834 use. H. L. Mencken (*American Language*, 4th ed., Supp. I, p. 181) provides only the date 1865. All agree that it is now obsolete. The latest work on this subject, William Safire's *The New Language of Politics* (1972), does not even mention it.

recently founded Workingman's party ("the Workies"), although indeed this party never got far from New York City and didn't amount to much there. And in part it was for the purpose of emphasizing by contrast the life of luxury that Martin Van Buren, nicknamed Sweet Sandy Whiskers or the Red Fox of Kinderhook, was said to be living at the White House—the golden plates and golden forks, the champagne, the silken cushions, the footmen with English accents.

Easily the most successful of these was John W. Bear of South Bloomfield, Pickaway County, Ohio, billed as the Buckeye Blacksmith. He made 331 speeches in eight states and the District of Columbia. A man of no political experience, a natural wit, an inspired clown, Bear was a hit from the start. He loved the crowds he bellowed at. He welcomed hecklers and dared them to do their worst, knowing that they had been hired by the startled Democrats, who were fighting back feebly with their Rough Hewer associations. And when he found that he couldn't shout them down, he would plunge into the crowd and seek them out, offering to wipe up the field with them, something he was quite capable of doing. The frontiersmen, the backwoodsmen, loved it.

The Buckeye Blacksmith, of course, knew nothing about national affairs, banking proposals, federal aid to interstate communications systems, or the encroaching virus of tariff greed, and if anybody asked him about these matters, he ignored the question.

At first he used to wear his blacksmith's leather apron and simply *talk* about his trade from time to time, contrasting the sinewy, hard-working, honest blacksmith with the pampered, perfumed macaroni who lolled in the White House. Later, as his act grew surer and the crowds more appreciative of his efforts, his sponsors provided him with an anvil, bellows, a bag of charcoal, permitting him to act out the part right up there on the stage. He did this with glee. He would beat out a horseshoe and then hold up the white sputtering product in his tongs and pretend that he was about to toss it into the ranks of the faithful, or he would cry: "Folks, if'n you'll jist point him out, I'd like to nail this onto the behind of that jackass that called out hurrah for Martin Van *Ruin* a little while ago!" It always went over big.

John W. Bear made a very good thing of the campaign of 1840, earning enough to take reading and writing lessons as he went along, and when it was over, he indited his autobiography. It did not sell well.

A wretch named Chamberlain, billed as the Kinderhook Blacksmith, used to devote his time to the telling of stories, all scurrilous, about the President, whom he proclaimed as a fellow townsman. Nobody in Kinderhook, it turned out, had ever heard of him, but the campaign was over by that time anyway.

There was Elihu Burritt, the Learned Blacksmith, who delighted his listeners by salting the scandal he told with bits of Ovid—or what he said was Ovid. There was Longhead, the St. Louis Blacksmith, also Henry Wilson, the Natick Cobbler, and Tom Corwin, the Wagon Boy, who asserted that he had once worked, as a civilian driver, for General William Henry Harrison, folks, Old Tippecanoe himself, our next President!

There was also, among these minor virtuosi, a gangling young man from Illinois named Abraham Lincoln, who wore patched denims and was otherwise folksy. He was advertised as the Railsplitter, having once finished first in a rail-splitting contest. He had a high, rather squeaky voice and was not prepossessing, but his imitations of political opponents were lapped up by a crowd that always liked "locals." He never mentioned his party's principles, if any.

John Tyler, a Virginia gentleman unaccustomed to such shenanigans, shook a sad head. He was involved in a monumental eruption of pishtosh, and yet he felt he should take part in the slangwhanging, even if only briefly. He had been brought to this opinion by the belief that his new owners had every right to expect such an activity from him as nominee for the Vice Presidency; in other words, he conceived it to be his duty. The masterminds had planned to send him on circuit throughout the Ohio Valley as living proof that they represented every national interest, but his passage north was undistinguished and at times ridiculous, as he tried the evasive tactics he supposed were expected of him, squirming out from under the verbal attacks of his audiences. He was a man of impressive appearance, an open-faced man, frank and easy of manner, well trained in all the tricks of the political orator. But the hecklers who were waiting for him at every stop were well trained, too, and at last they cornered him. This was in Pittsburgh. Tyler was tired, perhaps desperate. When they demanded to know what he stood for, he hesitated an instant, for like Washington he simply could not tell a lie. He dismissed the question with a wave of his hand. "I am in favor of what General Harrison and Mr. Clay are in favor of," he quavered.

They laughed, the ruffians. It was the one thing he could not stand. Cutting short his trip, he returned to Virginia, where he sat out the rest of the campaign in a dignified silence.

It was quite a different story when the Presidential candidate himself, William Henry ("Old Tip") Harrison, decided to become a slangwhanger.

Here was something for which there was no precedent. No President or Presidential nominee ever before had asked the public for votes, either for himself or his party. It simply wasn't done. American Presidential candidates always "stood" for office, like their English cousins; they did not "run." True, President John Adams, a very volcano of words on every occasion, once in New Jersey, on his way from the capital to his beloved Braintree, Massachusetts, paused long enough to get off a few paeans of praise for John Adams, but he did not actually remind his hearers that he might be running (or standing) for reelection, and the words seemed mere verbal fireworks so characteristic of this man. John Quincy Adams, too, fancied himself as a polished orator—although this was not an opinion shared by all—and even he, and even the current chief magistrate, Martin Van Buren, did not dream of uttering a first-person campaign speech, which would have been unspeakably conceited, barbarous, and out of keeping with the speaker's condition. To be sure, most of them were miserable talkers in the first place, ill at ease on a platform, mumblers, whose words could not be heard beyond the third row. Washington, Jefferson, Madison, Monroe, and Andrew Jackson hated formal delivery and avoided it whenever they could.

Not so William Henry Harrison. He was a candidate who had no intention of keeping the accustomed quietude. He knew as well as the next man, as well as any of his predecessors, that tradition called for a stern, impartial silence on his part. But he was human, and he loved to hear applause. June 6 of that fateful year, from the steps of the National Hotel, Perrysburg, Ohio, on his way to a celebration on the anniversary of the Battle of Fort Meigs at Columbus, the general—without any preparation, without professional assistance—delivered the first Presidential candidate's campaign speech. He urged his listeners to vote for him. And the heavens did not fall.

The speech was not long—it was curt by current standards, a bare hour—but they enjoyed it. They cheered and cheered.

Back East, the masterminds, hearing of this, were frantic with fear. They should have built a cage for this candidate and kept him in it until inauguration time. There was nothing that they could do now. He was already receiving invitations to speak elsewhere in Ohio, and accepting them with unseemly alacrity. He was to make more than twenty such addresses.

General Harrison had no wit. He couldn't sing or do imitations or manufacture a horseshoe on stage. But he loved the work, the sudden upswarming of applause, and glowed in the knowledge that he could sway a crowd. He was no pioneer, no adventurer or groundbreaker. He stuck to the time-honored topics, resoundingly endorsing mother love and lower taxes, not to mention the good old red-white-and-blue. He stood, in fact, foursquare for whatever he thought his audience would like to hear, although his favorite subject was himself, a person for whom he entertained a very high admiration. Time and again he told the story of Tippecanoe and of the Thames, and how he had whupped the redskins.

Harrison had very little education. He was not even a lawyer. He had attended no sort of school or academy, much less college, although he did suffer through a few lessons in Roman history at home under a tutor. He would refer to these from time to time, but he simply didn't know enough about the subject to bore his listeners, and he never did quote Latin at them, for he couldn't. Instead, he harped upon how highly he had valued the men who fought under his command, and how when the Indian campaign was over, he shook each of them by the hand and begged him to drop in any time he got near North Bend, Ohio, where, he would add, the latchstring was always out. They liked this. They sang:

"Old Tip he wears a homespun coat.
He has no ruffled shirt-wirt-wirt.
But Mat he has the golden plate,
And he's a little squirt-wirt-wirt."

3

★ ★ ★

That Great Log Cabin in the Sky

Newspaper editor Thurlow Weed, like Shakespeare's Autolycus, could be called a snapper-up of unconsidered trifles. When William Learned Marcy was running for governor, it was Weed who found in the record of this candidate what might have been—what almost was—a fatal flaw. Marcy was one of the ablest of the Albany Regency—a clique of upstate New York Democrats, considered the country's first political machine, whose leader was Martin Van Buren—and it looked as if he would have his own way at the election, for the Seward-Weed crowd had nobody strong to oppose him. Then Weed pulled this rabbit out of a hat—and everything was changed.

Two years before, when Marcy was a New York Supreme Court justice, he had submitted a bill for expenses while on circuit, as allowed by law. An item in that bill was

50 cents to a tailor for "repairs to my trousers." Nobody else would have noticed it. Weed did.

It was not that he smelled fraud—Marcy was scrupulously honest—but this saturnine newspaperman knew that you could do wonders with a word like "pants," if you were sure of your facts. Soon his Albany *Evening Journal* was thundering: Do you want as your next governor a man who charges the taxpayer for a patch in his pants? who gets a salary of $2,000 a year—yes, $2,000!—yet stoops to scooping 50 cents out of the public treasury?

Weed was violating no libel law. The expense-account item was perfectly legitimate: the judge actually had torn his trousers—on a nail that should not have been there—as he climbed to one of his benches, in other words, in the course of his duty. But the news of it made the electorate laugh, and a laughing voter is an unpredictable voter. Marcy won the election, though by a close vote, and he went on to the United States Senate, but he was never able quite to quell from his ears the echoes of that laughter. He never was able to live down "the patch in Marcy's pants."

It is not argued here that Thurlow Weed, who shunned personal publicity, was the genius who pounced upon the phrase "hard cider and log cabin," but he *could* have been. It was somebody *like* him, some follower, trained in Weed's journalistic school.

The story is familiar. A Democrat sneered at the nominee of the Whig convention: "Give him a barrel of hard cider and settle a pension on him, and, my word for it, he will sit the remainder of his days in his log cabin by the side of a 'sea coal' fire, and study moral philosophy." That did it. Within minutes Weed or whoever it was had started to spread the word; and the very name of the campaign became Log Cabin and Hard Cider.

The sneerer had made certain slips. William Henry Harrison, when he drank at all, preferred cognac brandy, and it is not likely that he had ever even sampled hard cider, a countryman's tipple. He was already making $6,000 a year. Why would he go to the expense of importing sea coals when he had more than 2,000 acres, much of it still wooded, and a small army of farmers to clear it? The reference to moral philosophy is puzzling. General Harrison, when he did get a chance to read, usually read books about Roman history.

The log cabin is the key to the whole thing. General Harrison's two-story clapboard house of seventeen rooms (not counting the stables, servants' quarters, barns, and other outbuildings), all set in the middle of an elaborately landscaped plot, surely could not be called a log cabin. But—perhaps it *had been?* This was possible, even probable. The log cabin was not a new concoction. It had been used in Scandinavia and northern Germany long before the discovery of America, although it was never known in Great Britain or the Low Countries. It had always been a more or less temporary shelter, a storehouse and toolhouse for seasonal hunting or working parties, and it kept this character when some Swedes and a handful of Finns brought the idea to the New World in 1638 and peppered the lower Delaware valley with these uncomfortable but sturdy structures. New Sweden did not last long, but the notching skill continued, passed from father to son, in those parts, and when George Washington planned to spend a winter at Valley Forge, Pennsylvania, he had no trouble getting directions for the creation of houses—"hutting" in official orders. The men were split into squads of twelve, each squad assigned to make one hut 14 by 16 feet, 6 feet 6 inches high, the sides and ends of logs, the roof of planks, the floor dirt, the chimney local fieldstone chinked with mud. The first of these was finished by the end of the second day, its builders winning a prize of twelve dollars, Continental paper, but it was weeks before the second was finished and some of them never really were. The Valley Forge huts were cold, leaky, smoky. The men hated them. The roofs were the worst, being too heavy and highly inflammable. Washington, who had been unable to get Congress to do this, offered $100 out of his own pocket to anybody who could invent or discover a better roofing material, but there were no takers.

After the war the poor and those who felt crowded pushed west, where log cabins began to appear. As before, these structures were looked upon as temporary. They were set up to provide shelter while the land was being cleared. They would not be torn down afterward, but rather built over, built around, each made to serve as the nucleus of a large and more substantial dwelling. This was their purpose in life on the frontier. No man who lived in a log cabin thought of it as an old homestead—heaven forbid! Such a man never dreamed, even fleetingly, that there would come a time when he would *boast* of having been brought up in a log cabin. They were not decorated, these stopgaps, but neither were they allowed to crumble into nothingness. They ended, usually, as a servant's room off the kitchen, or as a part of the kitchen itself, sometimes as a sort of tool shed, a lean-to. They were never looked upon as a symbol of America's humble beginnings—until 1840.

The hard cider might be more difficult to fit in. Many of the managers did not even know what the stuff was.

Anything like applejack? But at least it was not expensive and might be dished out with a free hand.

Also, "hard cider" would fit nicely into the songs the hacks had already started to grind out for marchers in the parades to come. This one, for instance, was titled "Gold Spoons and Hard Cider":

In a cabin made of logs,
By the river side,
There the Honest Farmer lives,
Free from sloth and pride.
To the gorgeous palace turn,
And his rival see,
In his robes of regal state,
Tinsell'd finery.

At the early morning light,
Starting with the sun—
See the farmer hold the plow
'Til the day is done.
In his silken bed of down
Martin still must be;
Menial servants waiting round,
Dress'd in livery.

See the farmer to his meal
Gayfully repair;
Crackers, cheese, and cider too,
A hard but homely fare.
Martin to his breakfast comes
At the hour of noon;
Sipping from a China cup
With a golden spoon.

Songs, songs! They were poured out by the dozen, by the score, on sheets, in handbooks, so as to be everywhere available. "General Harrison was *sung* into the Presidency," the elegant Philip Hone, ex-mayor of New York, was to complain in his diary.

> We've tried your purse-proud lords,
> Who love in palaces to shine.
> But we will have a ploughman
> President of the Cincinnati line.

In truth, the Whig candidate probably didn't know one end of a plow from the other, but what of that? The image was a good one, and to make it even better, the Democratic candidate, that hardworking country boy from Kinderhook, New York, must be made to appear the very epitome of effete Easternism, a sybarite, a voluptuary.

> What has caused this great commotion, motion, motion,
> Our country through?
> It is the ball rolling on, on,
> For Tippecanoe and Tyler too—Tippecanoe and Tyler too.
> And with them we'll beat little Van, Van, Van,
> And with them we'll beat little Van.

Above all, whether singing or speechifying, the hurrah boys must avoid any mention of unemployment, the national banking system, foreign relations, the tariff, the sale of public lands.

The Democrats fought back, if without much imagination. They hired shoulder-hitters to try to break up Whig rallies, at least around the edges, and men with the voice of Stentor to shout embarrassing questions at the Whig speakers. When one side started a whispering campaign to the effect that Van Buren was secretly a Roman Catholic, the other set up a counter-fire to the effect that General Harrison had sired many a Winnebago baby. (Both charges, being baseless, flopped.) The Democrats, when they were not too busy trying to tell the electorate what it was all about—and learning that the electorate didn't care—resurrected some of the old Andrew Jackson songs, particularly "Hickory Wood" and "The Battle of New Orleans." (The first of these has faded from the political repertory, but "The Battle," with different words, is popular still as "Hail to the Chief"), but these were not written for the occasion, as was

Farewell, dear Van.
You're not our man
To guide the ship.
We'll try Old Tip.

or:

With Tip and Tyler
We'll bust Van's b'iler.

Or this gem, written for singing on Saint Patrick's Day in a play for the Irish immigrant vote with which until this time the Whigs had scorned to flirt:

Here's to our fathers and mothers,
Likewise to ould Ireland too.
Down with Martin Van Buren,
And up with Tippecanoe.

The log-cabin float for such an occasion of course would be decorated with green paper shamrocks.

The songs, lest they be lost to history, were printed in many forms, nowhere more effectively than in the *Log-Cabin Song-Book,* a collector's item today, brought out by one of Thurlow Weed's oddest and most promising protégés, young Horace Greeley, who edited for the Albany Kingmaker his sensational New York City weekly *The Log Cabin*. *The Log Cabin* was called by no less an authority than Henry Raymond, "the most successful campaign sheet ever published." After the election Greeley was to change it to a daily, renaming it the *New York Tribune*.

Always the log cabin, in its most simplified form, was featured. Whig headquarters in any town would be in the form of a log cabin, erected for the occasion or else clapboarded with split logs to make it look like a real cabin. Pictures of log cabins were on handbills, on posters, everywhere you looked. A respectable Philadelphia distillery, E. G. Booz, even put out, specially for the campaign, whiskey bottles, pocket size, more or less in the shape of log cabins, the chimney being the mouth.* Every other float was dominated by a would-be replica of the frontiersman's first home, complete with coonskin nailed to the door, the latchstring conspicuously dangling therefrom, a jug marked "HARD CIDER," a plow in the front yard, and likely as not real smoke coming out of the chimney. The smoke, which emerged in unrealistic puffs,

*Gunderson, *The Log-Cabin Campaign,* p. 129. However, it was not from this firm's name that "booze" came into the language, as popularly reported at the time. "Bouz" or "bouse," also "bowse," go back to early in the eighteen century. Grose, *Classical Dictionary of the Vulgar Tongue*.

always brought a cheer from the sidewalks. Following this, lumbrously, would be a float depicting the effete and unfortunate villain of the piece, Sweet Sandy Whiskers, who (that dapper man!) was done up in clownish costume, clashing colors, as he lolled amid cushions supposed to be of silk. Matty Van on these floats always held in one hand a bottle on the label of which the word "CHAMPAGNE" was large enough to be read from a considerable distance. (Actually, Van Buren did not much care for champagne, preferring the red still wines of Bordeaux, his favorites being Margaux and Lafite.)

> Let Van from his cooler of silver drink wine,
> And lounge on his cushioned settee.
> Our man on a buckeye bench can recline,
> Content with hard cider is he.

Alongside this float, marchers, often children if it was not a night parade, would chant "Van, Van, is a used-up man!" This was done in order to anticipate voter objections to General Harrison as too old for the job. The Used Up theme occurred in many songs. It was coupled with the Me Too image. But Martin Van Buren's *record* was never examined, or even mentioned.

The Tip and Ty Kids were not the first to be exploited by politicians. There had sprung up in Baltimore at about this time, just before the start of the campaign, an organization of reformed drinking men who called themselves, no one knows why, the Washingtonians. These, America's first disciplined drys, took no part in party politics but favored rather a great deal of public talk about the evils of alcohol. At rallies they featured the Horrible Example, exhibiting on a platform the town drunkard, made to look even more repulsive than usual. The Washingtonian movement, conceived in a saloon, was virtually leaderless, and it lasted only a few months, but in that time it enlisted thousands of pledge signers and spread all over the East, particularly in the cities, where it staged elaborate parades. Very suddenly it ceased to exist, largely, men said, because its hullaballoo was drowned out by the hullaballoo of the Whigs, who were just then getting under way.

The Washingtonians had two branches, neither well organized. Martha Washingtons were of course a ladies' auxiliary. They used to get right out and march with the men, a shocking performance that was greeted, often enough, by the advice that they go home to their husbands, where they belonged. The other branch was the Cold Water Army, which consisted of whatever sons of Washingtonians could be rounded up for the occasion, and taught to sing, taught, too, to keep in step. They were all supposed to be "saved" children—that is, the offspring of reformed (just in time) drunkards. They wore blue-and-white uniforms, and each carried a tiny American flag. Sometimes they sang a song called "Dash the Bowl to the Ground," the composition of a distinguished Washingtonian, the Reverend John Pierpont, whose grandson, J. Pierpont Morgan, was to go far in the banking business. More often they confined themselves to the simpler and probably more effective chant:

> We'll purify the ballot box
> We'll consecrate the ballot box,
> We'll elevate the ballot box
> When we are twenty-one.

This was about as near as any Washingtonian ever got to expressing a political thought in public, and it was to be imitated almost immediately by the Whigs of 1840 with their bright boys who accompanied the floats, chanting, "Van, Van, is a used-up man!"

Since that time neither party has gone in heavily for child labor. Women, however, are something else.

Until 1840 it was assumed that a woman's place was in the home and that politics was a man's business. The Harrison Ladies and the Log Cabin Belles changed all that. Mostly they were busy with the clambakes and barbecues, doing the hard work; but they were known, too, to march in the parades, plugging along next to the lumbrous glittering floats, holding aloft sputtering torches, and doggedly chanting the belittlement of Martin Van Buren. Nor were they hooted at, jeered, as the Martha Washingtons had been, as the suffragettes were to be.

Men, women, and children, then, all America seemed to be enwrapped in politics, regardless of what, if anything, the real issues were. They sang, they cheered, they ate and drank, and time and again they assured one another and all passersby that Tip and Ty would prove winners. If occasionally they stumbled in their impetuous pace, it was because they had fixed their gaze too intently upon that Great Log Cabin in the Sky and nothing else mattered.

Harrison won.

4

★ ★ ★

"Killed Them as Dead as Smelts"

Harrison won; but it was a victory that established no record, and it should not have been called (as it was) a landslide.

It took a long time for the returns to come in, but there were no regional upsets. The balloting for electors was stretched over three weeks. In Ohio and Pennsylvania, early birds, it took place October 30, but in eleven other states not until November 2, and some elections were held later in November, in Rhode Island and South Carolina as late as the twenty-third.

By 1840 sixteen of the twenty-six states had eliminated all property and taxpaying restrictions on the suffrage, and the others had greatly reduced those restrictions. The popular vote was big, as expected: it was 54 percent higher than that of 1836. Harrison got 234 electoral votes,

Van Buren only 60, but the totals were 1.275 million and 1.128 million. Van Buren, though he lost, actually received 400,000 more votes than he got in '36. The Whigs, who had already controlled the House, won the Senate as well, though by a very slim majority.

The election, that is to say, had been a much closer thing than at first it seemed; and when the Whigs began to talk about the clear mandate they had received, Silas Wright, a sarcastic Senator from New York, snorted that their only mandate was to tear down the Capitol and build a log cabin in its place.

That at least the 1840 campaign *did* settle. Though the log cabin never did replace the white residence at 1600 Pennsylvania Avenue, it did become accepted as the symbol of the Presidency. No candidate could be complete without it.

Even the most fervent of the rah-rah boys did not pretend to believe that William Henry Harrison had been born in a log cabin. He was born, undeniably, in the family manor house at Berkeley on the James, Charles City County, Virginia. In 1796, while a captain in the army and commanding officer at Fort Washington (the present Cincinnati), having just married, he bought from his father-in-law—Judge John Cleves Symmes, a sensationally successful land speculator—the two-story, five-room house at North Bend. This structure was, in fact, built around and over a small log cabin. Harrison moved to Vincennes in 1800, but a few years later he returned to his North Bend purchase and modernized it. He made it over, with clapboards, shingles, all the rest, at the same time putting up a large number of outbuildings and increasing the size of the property from 400 to 2,800 acres, most of it along the river. There could be no doubt that he meant to live there for the rest of his life, having then no dream of occupying the White House. After he had in fact taken off for Washington and immortality as the ninth President of the United States, proud relatives, who were acting as caretakers of the Ohio estate, actually did tear some of the plaster off one of the walls in a downstairs bedroom, near the kitchen, to show that there was indeed a lining of notched logs. This aperture was permitted to stay that way for many years and was shown to sightseers.

The original building, including the hidden logs, was burned to the ground in 1858 when a steamboat pilot steered too close to the bank in order to give the passengers a good look, and sparks flew from her double black stacks.

Meanwhile, back in Washington, the most intense excitement prevailed. After all the tumult and the shouting, what would the new Chief Executive be like? What did he stand for? Was he really as old as they said? The politicians of Washington, D.C., like all gamblers everywhere, like sailors or actors, are a superstitious lot; and when William Henry Harrison arrived in the capital city February 9, his sixty-eighth birthday, in a raging blizzard, there were dark predictions about his future. He did look very old, men said.

Living in a hotel, he appointed his Cabinet, or agreed to its appointment by representatives of Mr. Clay. Daniel Webster was to get State. (There never had been any doubt of this—nobody in the know for a moment supposed that $63,000 had been the whole of Webster's slangwhanging fee.) Thomas Ewing of Ohio was to get the Treasury, John Bell of Tennessee the War Department, George C. Badger of North Carolina the Navy,

Francis Granger of New York the Postmaster Generalship, and Judge J. J. Crittenden of Kentucky the Attorney Generalship. Except for Webster and possibly Badger, these were all Henry Clay adherents.

Clay himself, a Senator now, came back to Washington, prepared to crack his whip, if necessary, prepared to take over the government in the name of his American System. A volatile man, he had recovered from his rage at learning of his rejection by the Harrisburg convention, and he was all bustling optimism, if a bit overbossy.

The President-elect too was busy. It was known that he was composing his inaugural address, which would certainly contain a great many references to Roman history, and which, it was feared, would go on and on. Men wondered whether so old a man could get through so heavy a speech, and Daniel Webster was quietly assigned to the task of reading the thing and cutting it down—way down. Webster took the job seriously, as he took everything. He came home to his rooming house one night after working late at his temporary office, and his landlady, Mrs. William W. Seaton, was alarmed by his appearance. He looked haggard, she said. Had anything happened? "You would think that something had happened if you knew what I have just done," replied the Secretary of State-Elect. "I have killed seventeen Roman proconsuls as dead as smelts."

Despite this massive deletion the speech ran long. It took General Harrison more than an hour to deliver it. The ceremony, as it had been from the time of Andrew Jackson's first swearing-in, was performed out of doors, and all the time there was a cold, relentless rain, so that the bareheaded oath-taker was soaked. Again the superstitious Washingtonians shook their heads, clucked their tongues; and, sure enough, a few days later the new President began to cough.

The cough grew worse. After a while the President, obviously weak, protesting that he was too busy to spare the time, went to bed. It was a bed from which he was never to rise. Four weeks from the time when he had been inaugurated, almost to the day, he died.

5

★ ★ ★

Hard Feelings on the Potomac

Daniel Webster, the Archangel, had no objection to nepotism. He had searched the Constitution diligently before he decided that it was all right for him to appoint relatives to office, a privilege most politicians took for granted. It was a son of the Secretary, Fletcher Webster, chief clerk of the State Department, who was told to take the news to John Tyler.

Tyler, bored with his Vice-Presidential existence in Washington, where there was nothing for him to do now that the Senate was not in session, had retired to his not at all palatial home in Williamsburg, Virginia. It was there that young Webster, accompanied by a Mr. Beall, an officer of the Senate, found him—at five o'clock in the morning.

Tradition has it that Tyler and his three sons were on

their knees on the living-room floor playing a game of marbles. This has become a myth, not to be shaken by mere facts, such as, for example, the fact that the Vice President was notoriously a late riser, the fact that 5 A.M. is scarcely a suitable time, nor the living room a suitable place, for marbles, or the facts that Tyler's two older sons, married and with households of their own, lived elsewhere, while the youngest was away at college. No matter. This is the way the scene has been painted.

They had breakfast, and John Tyler said good-bye to Letitia, and then they set forth for Washington. By boat and horseback, without pause, they made the 230 miles in twenty-one hours, a record.

They might have saved themselves the trouble. The capital was not ready for them. Once again the leaders of this nation were lost when they learned that the Founding Fathers had made no provision for the lesser half of a "balanced ticket"* succeeding because of death, and they were in a state of pitiful bewilderment.

Just as the Fathers had made no provision for political parties, not even a *mention* of them, so they had left the matter of succession in the air, writing only: ". . . in case of the removal of the President from office, or of his death, resignation, or inability to discharge the powers and duties of the said office, the same shall devolve on the Vice-President."

Now, did "the same" refer to "the office" or to "the duties"? Learned statesmen everywhere were asking themselves this question. Even so distinguished a Constitutional attorney as Daniel Webster, the Secretary of

*As one orator, John Siston, put it: "Tip was Bank, Ty was anti-Bank; Tip was tariff, Ty was anti-tariff; Tip was Distribution, Ty was anti. In fact, Fellow citizens, Tip is Whig, Ty is Democrat." Chitwood, *John Tyler*, p. 194.

State, was asking it as he hurried to Brown's Indian Queen ("the Wigwam"), the hotel where John Tyler had taken rooms. So were the other Cabinet members.

Tyler, always the gentleman, greeted them one by one, and thanked them for coming, and asked them if they would continue to serve as Cabinet secretaries. One by one, startled, uncertain of themselves, they said that they would.

Most of these men, all indeed excepting Webster and the Postmaster General, Granger of New York, were adherents of Henry Clay, and Clayites were not supposed to make up their minds on any sort of issue until they had received instructions from the chief. Traditionally the President is the head of his party, but was Tyler in fact the President or was he only a sort of regent, a suffragan, a caretaker? One thing at least was certain: He was not Mr. Whig. That was, and could only be, Henry Clay, who was not present at the Indian Queen conference.

The Archangel, though surely not shy, could be secretive sometimes in matters like this—matters, that is, in which his opinion had not been paid for. What he really thought of Henry Clay and of John Tyler must be locked forever in history's bosom; but it is tolerably certain that at the Indian Queen he harbored still some vague thought of controlling Clay's own Cabinet (as of course it really was) as its senior member, its most distinguished ornament, its doyen. That this amiable Virginian might become in fact the full-time, undisputed President, Webster did not for a moment believe; and if these Secretaries here assembled were in truth to rule the nation in Tyler's name, he, Daniel Webster, meant to rule *them*. Clay would continue to run the Whig party, which now controlled both houses of Congress. Black Dan, though he hated the chief, grudgingly granted that Clay was the only man capable of administering that post; a lot could be done in four years by one who held the reins of executive power—and knew how to use them. William Henry Harrison before he died had promised that he would not stand for re-election when his term ran out; and until this terrible thing had happened at the White House it was assumed by all interested parties that Henry Clay was as good as guaranteed the Presidency when 1844 came around. Webster, however, was thinking different thoughts.

He was quickly disillusioned.

Harrison had died at 12:30 Sunday morning, April 4. Tyler got to Washington a little before 5 A.M. Tuesday, and immediately started to look around for a Supreme Court justice who would swear him in as President. The court was not in session, and the only justice available was Roger Taney (pronounced Tawney), a resident of Baltimore. Taney, the Chief Justice, liked long black cigars. He had been appointed by Andrew Jackson to succeed the seemingly ineradicable John Marshall, and he did not trust John Tyler, an anti-Jackson Democrat who had gone over to the Whigs. He refused to go to Washington to administer such an oath unless he was "officially" requested to do so. What he meant by "officially" he didn't say, and there was no time for further hairsplitting. William Cranch, chief judge of the circuit court of the District of Columbia, who lived in Washington, was summoned to the Indian Queen, where he gave it as his opinion that, as Tyler himself believed, the Vice-Presidential oath Tyler already had taken would be sufficient, although Judge Cranch agreed that it could do no *harm* to administer the real, the full Presidential oath of office; and this was done.

April 7 the funeral was held, with Tyler prominent as a pallbearer.

April 9 the new Chief Executive issued a statement to the people of the United States, a statement he clearly meant to be taken in lieu of an inaugural address. It was evasive, calculated to placate Clay and his followers, and though written with care, not up to the literary standards of this William and Mary graduate, which were high. Nevertheless, it was hailed as a masterpiece by most of the Whig newspapers.

April 13 Tyler issued a proclamation setting aside Friday, May 14, as a day of fasting and prayer for the late plowman.

April 14 he moved into the White House.

He was accompanied—but very quietly—by his ladywife, the lovely Letitia, about whom nobody in Washington was to learn much, for she was a dim figure and distant, an invalid who stayed in an upstairs bedroom, away from the public rooms of the White House, mythlike, shimmering softly, not even a far-off voice, and a smattering of their seven children, those who were not in college or visiting relatives at the time. It was a hushed household, for Letitia was expected to die any day.

John Tyler was the youngest man ever to become President.* He took the oath of office exactly six days after his fifty-first birthday anniversary.

He *looked* like a President, the only one since Washington who had.

It was Daniel Webster, the self-appointed spokesman for the Cabinet, who made it clear to Mr. Tyler, at the first regular meeting in the White House, how the Secretaries felt about their status in the executive department. Gen-

*He was to hold this distinction until September 14, 1901, when Theodore Roosevelt, aged forty-one, succeeded the assassinated William McKinley. John F. Kennedy was forty-four in 1960, the youngest man ever to be *elected* President.

eral Harrison, he related, in the short while that he had presided here, had been wont to poll them individually for their opinions on every important question, and then to vote with the majority. Mr. Tyler shook his head. No, he said. He was polite, as always, and he made it clear that he valued their separate opinions and would respect and consider them; but the actual decision in every case, he finished, would be his own.

Even the voluble Black Dan had nothing to say about this; but they must all have wondered what Mr. Clay would think.

There were now three living ex-Presidents of the United States. Martin Van Buren was back in his native New York, repairing political fences, working his acclaimed wizardry on the masses, a distinguished citizen though not an elder statesman, an activist to be sure and not at all the "used-up man" the Whig paraders had proclaimed: he was still in his fifties, and looking toward 1844. Andrew Jackson spluttered almost unnoticed down in the Hermitage, near Nashville, Tennessee, a firecracker that might yet explode, a thing to keep away from. John Quincy Adams, the crustiest of them all, was in the House of Representatives, where he made many momentous speeches—he was called Old Man Eloquence—although he saved the cream of his acerbity for his diary, written, in Van Wyck Brooks's words, "with malice toward all, with charity for none." Adams' diary was not published in his lifetime, which is just as well. It would have caused a greater explosion than any Tennessee firecracker. For this irascible old man could write of "the gigantic intellect, the envious temper, the ravenous ambition, and the rotten heart of Daniel Webster." He could write: "He [William Henry Harrison] is not the choice of three-fourths of those who have elected him. His present popularity [December 4, 1840] is all artificial. There is little confidence in his talents or his firmness." He had no use, either, for Harrison's successor:

> Tyler is a political sectarian, of the slave-driving, Virginian, Jeffersonian school, principled against all improvement, with all the interests and passions and vices of slavery rooted in his moral and political constitution—with talents not above mediocrity, and a spirit incapable of expansion to the dimensions of the station upon which he has been cast by the hand of Providence, unseen through the apparent agency of chance.

John Quincy Adams was a smallish man, prickly as a porcupine, a Puritan of Puritans, who looked as if he carried vinegar in his mouth instead of spit, and who saw the world as all black and white, mostly black, but with no grays. His diary, "the vast treasure-house of damnations which Adams left," is a delight. He wrote it only after dark, as a proper diarist should do, and on the night of April 16, 1841, he wrote: "I paid a visit this morning to Mr. Tyler, who styles himself President of the United States, and not Vice-President acting as President, which would be the correct style."

J. Q. Adams, never one to run with the crowd, here had hit a popular note. Many others were wondering, too, how the new President—if he really *was* the President—should be addressed. John Tyler, by his decision to assume instantly the full duties and responsibilities of the office, had in effect written a new clause into the Constitution, a clause that the Fathers had left unwritten. He had established an important precedent, but he had done nothing to stabilize the official salutation. "His Accidency" was often suggested, not always in a playful way, although it is not on record that anybody ever accosted him to his face as "*Your* Accidency," and Tyler, had this been done, undoubtedly would have ignored the rudeness.

Could a man in truth be President who had never been *elected* President? This was a question that perplexed even the most expert hairsplitters in Washington. Did not such an upstepping foreshadow a sort of the-king-is-dead-long-live-the-king attitude—in other words, the divine right of royalty? Had not we ended all that when we won the war of the Revolution?

As a result of the Log Cabin and Hard Cider campaign, the Whigs had control of both houses of Congress, although in the Senate this control was very narrow. Henry Clay, back from a brief vacation in Kentucky, was in full charge on the Hill, and was eager to put through every part of his American System. With this in mind he had induced old General Harrison, during his short sojourn in the White House, to call a special session of Congress for May 31. This call was still in effect, His Accidency having done nothing to modify or redate it.

Henry Wise of Virginia in the House offered a resolution informing "the President of the United States," as John Tyler was "by the Constitution, by election, and by an act of God," that Congress was willing to receive communications from him. Immediately McKeon of New York was on his feet proposing an amendment to make this read "the Vice-President, now exercising the duties of—" but this was easily defeated, and Wise's original motion was carried.

The next day the Senate took up this momentous matter, when John W. Allen of Ohio moved that the man in the Executive Mansion should thereafter be officially addressed as "the Vice-President, on whom, by the death of the late President, the powers and duties of the office of

President have devolved," but this was voted down 38 to 8.

Personally, individually, the members of Congress, when they had occasion to visit the White House on business, solved the problem of salutation in different ways. Some—no doubt wincing inwardly as they did so—sternly stilled their hearts and used "Your Excellency" and "Mister President" to the man's face. Others gave him no sort of title. Still others, aware that John Tyler as governor of Virginia had once accepted the honorary designation of captain in order to assist a recruiting drive for the state militia—although he never had worn a uniform or served a day in the armed forces—seized upon this excuse to address him as "Captain." President Tyler seemed amused by this, but he made no comment.

A great change had come over Henry Clay, America's own Great Commoner, diplomat extraordinary, author and principal sponsor of the Missouri Compromise. Before the campaign of 1840, he had resigned from the House of Representatives, where he had served as speaker for many years, and returned to Ashland, his Kentucky plantation. Nobody took this "retirement" seriously. Clay was a political person, every inch of him, and it was assumed—correctly—that he would soon be back in the middle of it. When, thanks to the maneuvering of Thurlow Weed, et al., he was passed over by the Whig convention at Harrisburg, he had quickly recovered. He did little in the Log Cabin and Hard Cider campaign, for he was too honest a man to countenance evasion, and he still had the principles of his American System at heart; but as soon as it was over and the Whigs were in control of both houses of Congress, he had himself elected to the U.S. Senate and went back to the District of Columbia, where he belonged. He was, however, a different man.

Clay had always been a wonder child, even when grown up, a prodigy, to whom all things political came easy. Everybody who knew him loved him, even those who feared him. The secret of his power, it seemed at first, was largely personal. His grin was his most precious asset, his bonhomie his most efficient corraller of votes. Nobody could resist that famous amiability, and it was not often necessary for Henry Clay to push, for he could win his points without ever raising his voice. Always the friendly gray eyes twinkled, the freckles fairly popping out of his face.

Back from the somnolence of his estate, Ashland, he glowered. It was for the first time to many of his followers, and it confused them. Uncharacteristically he barked his orders. Today we would say that he had lost his cool. It seemed—although men in the big white building under the dome scarcely dared to whisper this among themselves—that the rejection at Harrisburg had hurt him more deeply than he would dare to admit. Gone was the camaraderie of old. He was touchy. He snarled.

Even William Henry Harrison, a complacent man, a man most anxious to please, revolted against this dictation. He had agreed readily enough to announce that in no circumstances would he stand for a second term as President. He agreed to many other things. But he got tired at last of listening to Henry Clay propound the terms under which he would lead his Congressional forces the President's way, and in a fit of recalcitrance he asked Mr. Clay not to come to the White House anymore unless and until he had some legitimate government business to discuss. Clay's feelings were hurt, for he considered this the grossest sort of ingratitude; but his prestige on the Hill seemed unimpaired.

The promise not to run again seemed to make secure

Henry Clay's claim to the nomination in 1844; and then General Harrison had to go and die, spoiling everything.

Harry of the West and His Accidency were old friends, good friends. The Great Compromiser, right away, told the President what he expected. They were having a whiskey.

First of all, Mr. Clay explained, the Bank of the United States was to be rechartered.

Mr. Tyler said no.

Mr. Clay, unaccustomed to hearing this word, bridled. Mr. Tyler was placatory. Granted, he said, he had agreed to run on the Whig ticket in the late loud election campaign, but he had never agreed to support a resurrection of the Bank of the United States. No. However, if Mr. Clay would make certain changes in his projected bill . . . Mr. Clay went back to his office, satisfied that everything was all right.

He tinkered with his bank bill, but not enough. He was warned that Mr. Tyler would never accept the result; but he pooh-poohed this, he tut-tutted it. "Tyler dare not resist," the new Henry Clay announced. "I will drive him before me."

So he pushed his bill through both houses, and it went to the White House, and President Tyler vetoed it.

Henry Clay no doubt roared with rage; but when he had ceased roaring, he went right back to work. He still controlled both houses of the national legislature, but in the Representatives the Whig majority was only 49; in the Senate, through which the bank bill had squeaked 25 to 24, it was only 7, so there could be no thought of a repassage over the veto. Clay started to tinker with the bill again, to make it acceptable to His Accidency.

This was a turning point in American history, this contest.

6

★ ★ ★

A President Without a Party

In the language of the time Clay was a nationalist, Tyler a localist. Tyler believed in states' rights, Clay believed that Congress was supreme. It was the old pull-apart between Thomas Jefferson and Alexander Hamilton, between the "implied powers" interpretation of the Constitution and the "exact words" version.

The Bank of the United States (BUS), despite that official-sounding name, was to have been a private corporation, a money company organized and authorized to handle the nation's fiscal affairs, including the issuance of paper money. The government was to hold one fifth of the stock in this company. The bank's powers were almost unlimited, although there was a limit to the charter under which it was created in 1791, and when in 1811 this expired, it was not renewed. The Virginians were in full charge of the government then, the Jeffersonians, and they wanted no part of a privately owned national bank. They would have dropped it earlier if they'd been able to do so constitutionally.

The country got along very well managing its own finances, for a while, until the War of 1812 threw everything out of kilter. It was a war that the United States never should have started, not being able to afford it. The nation was left deeply in debt and floundering on the very verge of bankruptcy, so that the Bank of the United States, though still unconstitutional in the eyes of the ruling Virginians, was restored. The new charter was limited to twenty years, as the original had been. It authorized a capitalization of $35 million, one fifth of it owned by the government, and a board of twenty-five, five of them appointed by the President, the rest elected by the stockholders. Thus, it was firmly fixed in selectivity, and not for the commons. At the end of 1829, for instance, when BUS was riding very high, more than a quarter of its $28 million of privately owned stock was in the hands of 383 foreigners, and of the remaining $20 million over $16 million, or more than half of the total not owned by the United States government, belonged to 822 individuals. The remaining 2,780 private American owners held a little more than $3 million of stock. The bank was easily the biggest corporation in the United States, and one of the biggest in the world.

The bank, everybody admitted, was a success—on paper. Monopoly or not, it did its job well. The brainchild of Alexander Hamilton—who got the idea, as he got so many of his ideas of government, from England, in this case from the Old Lady of Threadneedle Street (the Bank of England)—it had formed one of the four bases of his policy as first Secretary of the Treasury. Hamilton believed that to those who had should be given. The new nation, he explained, needed a fiscal system administered by experienced capitalists, bankers; and he did everything he could to get these personages financially interested in the venture. That nothing was said in the Constitution about a private company being placed in control of the nation's finances he brushed aside as a matter amply covered by the doctrine of implied powers. The Jeffersonians did not think that way.

Though Hamilton himself was long gone, a discredited politician, a business failure, and his Federalist party was dying at the end of the War of 1812, the rechartering of BUS was carried out without incident, and, as before, the thing worked. It was undemocratic; it might have been unconstitutional; but its figures came out right. The Jeffersonians, necessarily, endured it. They could not look to the judicial branch of the government in hope of relief, for the judicial branch—only three Supreme Court justices then—had been so packed by President John Adams just before his term ran out that it would go on blocking the Jeffersonians and undoing their work for many years to come. The Federalist party was dead, yes, but the justices of the Supreme Court, and especially Chief Justice Marshall, hidebound Federalists all, seemed immortal, inexpungeable.

The charter of the *second* Bank of the United States would expire in 1836, the last year of Andrew Jackson's second Administration. Jackson, the Hero of New Orleans, easily the most popular man in the nation, at first had declared himself opposed to a second term as President, but had changed his mind midway through the first—much to the consternation of the National Republicans, who were soon to become the Whigs. Henry Clay even then was thinking of himself as a Presidential nominee in 1836, and it was he, according to popular report, who persuaded the head of the Bank of the United States, the elegant Nicholas Biddle, to apply for a renewal of the charter several years in advance. Clay's idea, men said, was to have an out-and-out fight with the President, Old Hickory, who would certainly lose such a fight, leaving him, Henry Clay, the hero of the hour just as the new Presidential election campaign came along. Clay had talked to the rich men, and he believed that if properly guided they would be invincible. He would ride into office on the wings of his bank victory, and then he would inaugurate his American System step by step, starting with the renewal of the bank charter and the imposition of a high selective tariff, a process that would change the very nature of the United States government.

Clay underestimated his opponent. When Andrew Jackson fought, he fought not merely with his fingertips. Rather, he came in swinging with both firsts, as now, his chin down, his eyes blazing, and he did not desist until there was nothing left to hit. Jackson did not know the niceties of deficit spending, the delights of indebtedness, but he did know that out west, where he came from, the Monster of Chestnut Street* was pushing bank after state bank against the wall, insisting upon payment, and that the money this brought in went to a handful of Eastern and

*This designation, an obvious imitation of the Bank of England's Old Lady of Threadneedle Street, was applied to the gorgeous new structure in Philadelphia that was to serve as the headquarters and home base of the second Bank of America. One of the first of the Greek Revival buildings in America, and much pointed out, it was located on the south side of Chestnut Street between Fourth and Fifth Streets, one square east of Independence Hall.

European financiers, nobody else. He also knew that there was no provision in the United States Constitution for a national bank, which is why Thomas Jefferson had been opposed to it.

Jackson won. The battle, dry reading for students of American history today, was singularly exciting to all who participated in it or even watched from the sidelines. It had the whole country agog.

When Congress at last did pass a bill granting the second Bank of the United States a charter—and passed it by comfortable majorities—Andrew Jackson vetoed it.

The Presidential veto was still looked upon in Congress as an emergency measure, a brake to be applied only in cases of extreme peril, and even, according to Representative Samson Mason of Ohio, as a discountenanced British government trick:

> Is it not calculated to excite astonishment that one of the cast-off, disgraced, and obsolete prerogatives of the Crown of Great Britain should have been dug up from a dishonored grave, to which the indignant voice of that nation had consigned it, and borne across the Atlantic, to be transplanted in the soil of Republican America—here to be nourished and defended as "the tree of life" in our garden of Eden?

Nobody answered this, and the veto stood.

Old Hickory had seen to it that Martin Van Buren, his echo, was the regular Democratic nominee for President in 1836. Clay had run against him, and it had been a bitter fight, Van Buren winning by a hair—fewer than 30,000 out of the record 1.5 million votes cast.

Sweet Sandy Whiskers was not about to tolerate any renewal of BUS, not with General Jackson watching him from the Hermitage. He did what he could with his subtreasury plan, a well-thought-out compromise between the Jacksonians and the BUS extremists, but by the time he took over, the situation was already out of hand. The Bank of the United States, squirming and spitting in its death throes, had called in loans right and left, all through the West and the South. State banks out that way were in consequence closing down. They had been badly overextended and had issued great gobs of paper money backed by nothing. In a desperate effort to emulate New York and its lucrative Erie Canal, they had borrowed—mostly from Europe—almost $200 million, and now Michigan, Arkansas, Mississippi, and Florida had repudiated their debts outright, while others teetered on the verge. Prices soared. Andrew Jackson had been proudest of all of his record of paying off the national debt to the last penny; but now, only a few years after his retirement to Tennessee, this debt stood at some $7 million, the greatest yet, and it was rising in leaps and bounds. Van Buren did his best to stem the flood; but the Big Panic of 1837 ("panic" was the word then for what later generations would call "depression," and what today, under the guidance of the economists, we have learned to know as "recession") brought these efforts to smash.

General Harrison was known to be compliant to anything Mr. Clay asked or demanded, but General Harrison was not in office long enough to get anything done. As for His Accidency, though Mr. Tyler told Congress in his first message that the subtreasury system must go, and though when Congress had passed a bill to kill it, he promptly signed this, he was inflexibly opposed to a national bank of the Nicholas Biddle type, insisting rather upon what Andrew Jackson called "a branch of the Treasury Department." Tyler kept saying that he was open to argument, but it was not in Henry Clay's nature, just then, to argue. Clay laid down the law, admitting no exceptions, no modifications, until at last the President reacted as even General Harrison had done a little earlier under the same provocation. According to his own son, a witness to the scene, the courtly John Tyler rose from his chair in the White House and pointed up Pennsylvania Avenue: "Then go to your end of the capital and perform your duty as you think proper. So help me God, I shall do mine at this end—as I shall think proper." Clay left.

All of this might seem a matter of splitting hairs. It seemed so at least to Harry of the West. Clay saw the second Bank of the United States not as a device designed to make the rich richer, not as a Tory throwback, certainly not as the "hydra of corruption" Old Hickory had incautiously called it in his July 10, 1832, veto message. Rather he considered the Bank an institution absolutely necessary to keep the United States from drifting into chaos and bankruptcy. These men were sincere, both of them. They were patriots. Each was doing, with all his might, what he thought was best for the country.

Clay *did* come to believe that a few word changes in the bank law he proposed would make all the difference to His Accidency, who only sought to save face. He was mistaken in this, but it was an honest mistake.

Clay chipped away at the manhandled bill once again, prettying it up, as he supposed, rendering it more palatable to the fussy gentleman from Virginia, notably when he changed the word "bank" wherever it occurred to "fiscal corporation." Then, triumphantly, he put it through both houses of Congress, and it was sent to the White House—where John Tyler vetoed it again.

Thereafter it was war, nothing less. No longer were there projected any peacemaking conferences, no longer was there a show on the part of either side of any willingness to compromise. Now it was an out-and-out slambang fight, the kind of thing Andrew Jackson would have enjoyed. John Tyler was no Jackson, but he was no sissy either. His exquisite manners had fooled many men, including Henry Clay.

Resolutions were passed. Denunciations were thundered. At the White House there was a flood of letters threatening assassination. The very night of the day the veto message was signed—and the signing itself caused a near-riot in the Senate and the arrest of at least one spectator, who had hissed—a mob gathered outside the Executive Mansion, which was not then protected by any sort of wall or fence, and between midnight and two o'clock fired shotguns and blunderbusses, keeping up a down-with-Tyler shouting. This tumult awakened and greatly perturbed the lovely Letitia, victim of a paralytic stroke, who never left her bedroom in those days. The next night the President was burned in effigy on the far side of what is now Lafayette Square. The day after *that,* Henry Clay spoke in the Senate chamber for an hour and a half—laconic for him—and the speech, though filled with references to his "former friendship" with Mr. Tyler, was notably acidulous, undiplomatic, and in other respects deplorable. Clay capped it with a demand for a Constitutional amendment that would permit the overriding of a Presidential veto by a simple majority in each house of Congress. He was persuaded to withdraw this.

Rumors of impeachment proceedings swirled and writhed like so much fog; but these the President ignored.

Inside the legislative halls themselves, Tyler had precious few supporters, for even the Democrats were leery about coming to his aid. "A corporal's guard" Henry Clay had scornfully called the handful of Tyler men: George H. Proffit of Indiana, James I. Roosevelt of New York, Caleb Cushing of Massachusetts, and Henry S. Wise and Francis Mallory, both of Virginia. These were faithful to him.

Even his Cabinet walked out. This was a carefully planned mass resignation. The afternoon of Saturday, September 11, 1841, there should have been a Cabinet meeting at the White House, but instead of appearing for this, the various secretaries sent in their resignations, separately, by messenger. John Tyler, Jr., his father's private secretary, watch in hand, received and recorded them. In two days, on the Monday, Congress would adjourn. It was known that His Accidency did not believe in the validity of interim Cabinet appointments that had not been confirmed by the United States Senate, and it was assumed that he could not possibly, in that time, get up a Cabinet acceptable to the Senate. Thus he would be faced by the prospect of running the country for a good six months without any heads of departments, a task obviously impossible, and he would be forced to abdicate. As the setup then was, the double-accidency man who would succeed him was Samuel L. Southard, president of the Senate, a firm Clayite.

In other words, this looked like a knockout blow.

John Tyler was unruffled. As the presence of his watch-checking son-secretary attested, he had known of this plan. He had prepared against it. Instead of being crushed, he accepted the resignations politely, and filed them, and then announced a whole new Cabinet—with the exception of the Secretary of State, Daniel Webster, who remained. It was a Cabinet that even the Clay-controlled Senate could not reject.

Webster had come in person to the White House to offer *his* resignation, but he made it clear that he would do so only if the President requested this. Tyler asked him, instead, to stay, and Webster promptly agreed. He was afraid that this action would alienate him from the controlling Whigs, who were jumping through all sorts of hoops at the crack of the Clay whip, and he knew that the imperious boss, his eye still on the 1844 campaign, would take it as an evidence of his, Webster's, coming candidacy, but he had the legitimate excuse that his resignation at this time would have broken off the delicate negotiations he was conducting with the British ambassador Lord Ashburton about the Maine–Canada boundary.

Congress, about to expire, was not yet finished with the man in the White House. If he wouldn't abdicate, at least he must be castrated—politically speaking. On that same Saturday afternoon on which the Cabinet did not meet, a small group of extreme rightist Whigs did. They framed a manifesto addressed to the American people. They called a caucus of all Whig members of Congress to be held in Capitol Square the following Monday afternoon.

Many Senators and Representatives had already left Washington and its intolerable heat—the Dog Day Session, this had been called—assuming that there would be no important business on the last day of the special term. How many attended the caucus in Capitol Square is not known for certain—nobody seems to have counted them, and estimates range from fifty to eighty—but the vote was unanimous anyway. An address was issued to the American people repudiating His Accidency the Regent and all of his works and declaring that the "alliance" between him and the Whig party was at an end.

John Tyler had weathered the storm. He was still President. But he was a President without a party.

7

★ ★ ★

A Choice of Wars

"To a dog all the world's a smell." To the statesmen at Washington, that smell was power, specifically the Presidency. They sniffed it out the moment they came to the capital, and thereafter they thought of little else, certainly not of such minor matters as wives, children, and the good of the country. The scramble for the highest office was disgraceful. Almost everybody, it seemed, got into it, either as a candidate or as the friend of a candidate, for the role of Kingmaker was a popular one as well. In this respect, at least, they were virtually without conscience, and also without shame. As an early Christian would submit to any indignity his oppressors imposed upon him, any hardship or torture, even death itself, in the hope of getting into heaven, so the aspirants of the Millennium of the Minnows would stoop to almost any malpractice or mistreading in the hope of getting into the White House. They *thought* that they were whales, those earnest orators who thrashed about so noisily in the Congressional tank; but minnows in fact they remained. Perhaps the greatest of them, the redoubtable Henry Clay* (of whom it might be said, as Lemuel Gulliver said of the Emperor of the Lilliputians, that "he is taller by the breadth of my nail than any of his court, which is enough to strike an awe into the beholder") is remembered because of his remark, in a letter to his friend Senator Preston of South Carolina, that he would rather be right than President. But it is hardly to be thought that anybody at the time believed this.

That stately procession of staid responsible men, the Virginia Dynasty, who had passed the chief executiveship on to selected successors, usually the Vice President or the Secretary of State, no longer functioned. Now it was what the French call *sauve qui peut*, every man for himself, and this change of attitude, coming as it did at the same time as the establishment of the two-party system, had a telling effect upon American politics. The crown of Rome, first assumed by Augustus Caesar, was awarded each time to some son or nephew or other relative who had been carefully coached. But this system endured only through the first five of the emperors, after which the succession, once considered sacred, became a matter to be settled by dirty plot or assassination. So it was in Washington, where the methods employed, if not so criminal, were not a whit less unstatesmanlike.

It started with John Quincy Adams, whose accession to

*"Clay was essentially, constructively, triumphantly American. The impetuous impulse of Clay was to let the youth, the vigor, the creative spirit of triumphant America sweep in untrammeled activity whithersoever it would, secure that a beneficent providence would guide it. . . . And in all these various phases Clay embodied the spirit of the west . . . its nervous vigor, its all-attempting coverage, its undying enthusiasm." Bradford, *As God Made Them*.

the throne marked the end of the Era of Good Feeling, the beginning of the Great Grabfest. In 1820, when he was preparing to run for the top job—*run* for it, mind you, not *stand* for it—there were no fewer than eighteen other contestants. This field had been narrowed down to four at the time of the election: Clay, Adams, Andrew Jackson, and William H. Crawford. None of these got a majority of the electoral votes, and as the Constitution then provided, the top three, Crawford, Adams, and Jackson, were put before the House of Representatives, a body controlled by the fourth, Henry Clay, who saw to it that John Quincy Adams was elected—though Adams had not received as large a popular vote as Andrew Jackson. Soon after this Clay was appointed Secretary of State.

John Tyler liked to think of himself as a member of the Virginia Dynasty, the last of the line, perhaps, but definitely *there*. Why then did he not try to restore the proper gentlemanly procedure of his predecessors? Because he himself had joined the scramble, clawing at the greased pole. As we would say now, he suffered a severe attack of Potomac Fever. The moment he got into the White House, he started to make plans to be elected by one party or the other, conceivably by both, four years hence.

This would not be easy. The Whigs were angry with him, and likely to remain that way for a long time, and the Democrats were leery, esteeming him to be a traitor to their party. The Hero of New Orleans never stirred from the Hermitage these days and was the weakest kind of campaign orator anyway and not much of a letter writer, but his popularity was unabated. So, any disagreement with him was to true Democrats almost like a violation of the tenets bequeathed to America by Thomas Jefferson. The Hero still favored Martin Van Buren, his protégé, who was busy laying plans for a return to the White House. On the other side, Henry Clay, that model of affability, showed no sign of relaxing his rigidity on the bank issue and would be more anti-Tyler than ever as soon as he learned, as learn he must, that the gentleman from Virginia was aiming to retain a post Mr. Clay long had considered rightfully his. Clay indeed was the one predictable aspect of this confused situation. He could be counted upon to oppose with all his might—and block and confound—any man who aspired to the Presidency.

Something besides partisanship was needed, something in the nature of an emergency, which would bring the disparate sides together, uniting them behind Mr. Tyler. A war?

It must not be supposed that John Tyler deliberately sought to start a war in order to bolster his popularity. Far from it! He was a sincere lover of peace; and though he believed that the United States should have a strong army and navy, and worked to this end, he never did conceive of a nation that would try to jostle the other nations into line at command, teaching them a moral lesson the while, and most assuredly he never dreamed of himself as a saber-waving dictator. No. Foreign relations, to him, were the most fascinating facet of national administration; and diplomacy, as others had observed, was a gentleman's fit concern. He had always fancied himself as a diplomat. He was best equipped for this.

After much thought he chose Texas.

Texas was a porcupine, to be handled only with the most assiduous care. An area larger than France and reputed to be fertile, until recently it had been a state of Mexico, and it continued in this capacity after Mexico won her independence from Mother Spain. Texas, it would seem at a glance, had everything. A better look, however, revealed one serious lack—Texans. The church fathers from Iberia had never tried to populate the place through means of their missions, as they had done in California, north and south, upper and lower, and in New Mexico, which then included Arizona. There were a few wild Indians in Texas, but they seemed determined to stay wild. There was merely a sprinkling of Mexicans, most of them looking for a way to get out. Otherwise the province was sheer emptiness, the great open spaces. Higher-ups of Mexico City never visited it, for they feared to get that far from the capital, where a revolution might break out, ruining their careers, as soon as they turned their backs. Yet Texas *should* be settled, it should be exploited, for it would bring in tax money. Thus it was that the Mexican higher-ups, who were changed from time to time, made a deal with a Hartford, Connecticut, businessman named Moses Austin, who, having failed in many other fields, thought that he would try his hand at settlement. It was understood that any farmers he brought in would immediately become communicants of the Roman Catholic Church. It was also understood that they would abjure slavery, something that the Mexican Republic had only just legislated out of existence. The settlers—Moses Austin had died but his mild-mannered son took over the enterprise—were virtually all planters who were moving away from the worn-out cotton fields of the Deep South, and they naturally brought their slaves with them, knowing no other way to live. They hadn't the slightest intention of giving up those slaves, nor did they intend to pay even lip service, much less tithes, to the Catholic Church. Soon a revolution loomed. It could end, it would seem, only one way. There were six or seven million Mexicans, and they had a crack army; there were fewer than 50 thousand Texans, with no military organization at all. Nevertheless that vast stretch of mountain land and desert between Mexico City and the Rio Grande always had to be considered. When Santa Anna, the Gray Wolf of Mexico, who was also its current President, invaded Texas at the head of three thousand men, he knew that he had to get this job done in a hurry or he would have no home base left—such was the avidity of his political opponents. Santa Anna smashed and bayoneted the pitifully small garrison at the Alamo and he slaughtered in cold blood at Goliad some four hundred Texans who had surrendered to him on promise of lenity. By these acts he meant to cow the rebels. They had the opposite effect. If they scattered the Texans and sent them into a disorderly retreat, they also made them sore as hell. The news of such doings, circulating in the United States, raised a sea of sympathy for the struggling settlers and summoned to their aid great bands of godless but by no means gunless men, men who in many cases were no longer safe at home.

It also brought about cries in this country for intervention—full, official intervention, that is.

Washington had not been unaware of Texas, even before the shooting started. President John Quincy Adams and President Jackson had both instructed their diplomatic representatives in Mexico City to report on the possibility of a purchase. They did not take Mexico's national pride into consideration. Or her politics. Any government, even that of a dictator like Santa Anna, which allowed it to be known that it was dickering for the sale of Texas would be removed from office—instantly, violently.

San Jacinto changed all of that. The reassembled, reinforced Texans under stout Sam Houston smote the invaders hip and thigh at this remote spot, capturing Santa Anna himself, chasing the other survivors home.

Texas had already declared itself a republic, and now it asked the United States to take it in as a state. This, Mexico City warned, would mean war.

The United States did recognize the new republic, and so, soon afterward, did France, Great Britain, and Holland. But annexation would be a different matter. Annexation, even if it could somehow be managed without enraging the Mexicans, would exacerbate the slavery situation, the free-soil situation; it would threaten, again, a split. Like the tariff issue, the question of Texas tended to break the nation into two parts, North and South, and this would be bad for *everybody's* business.

The Texans, clearly, had no thought of freeing their slaves or even of laying long-distance plans for such an action. As they saw it, slavery was necessary to their continued existence; it was their very staff of life. Mexico, which still claimed Texas as a dependency, did not see it that way. Nor did the northern and eastern states of the American union, and most particularly New England, where the abolitionist sentiment was growing every day. Texas—the complaint was common even in those days—was just *too big*. Once admitted, it could be broken into two, three, even four separate states, and each of these would send its two Senators to Washington, where the balance of power would be tipped back in favor of the South. This, if it were to happen, inevitably would be met by a demand from the North that in order to restore equality, *all* of the disputed Oregon territory must be taken, clear up to the southernmost point of what the

Russians had settled. And indeed the cry of "Fifty-Four-Forty or Fight" already was loud in the land. This, in turn, could mean war with Great Britain.

John Tyler was especially susceptible to partisan carping in matters of this sort because of his known belief in states' rights, his conviction, which never wavered, that the state was sovereign and came first, that the only powers the federal union had over it were those specifically granted—and not just *implied*—in the Constitution. There had been no concealment of this belief. The Whigs had no excuse for pretending to be surprised by it. In speech after speech in both houses of Congress and also as governor of Virginia, Tyler made his opinion known, and he never qualified or amended it.

One of his first acts as Chief Executive was the signing of a new tariff bill sent him, with a snarl, by the Clay forces. He had done this, he protested, because the new rates, though high, probably were the best that could be obtained at that time, and also because the Treasury needed money and there seemed no other way to obtain this. His ex-associates the Democrats, however, denounced the deed as kowtowing to the nationalist, big-money, abolitionist Whigs, who, themselves, simply sniffed.

The Texas question was sure to be even touchier than the tariff question. Tyler approached it warily. Yet he *did* approach it. It could be that the slogans "Tyler and Texas" or alternatively "Texas and Tyler Too" were already knocking around in his ears. Whatever the reason, he determined to make the cause of annexation his own. He determined to have his Administration stand or fall on it.

Just as he had arrived at this decision, however, he was jolted by a reminder that he already had two wars on his hands, both of them north of Washington. Texas would have to wait.

8

★ ★ ★

Thunder over Narragansett Bay

Thomas Wilson Dorr was an earnest young man of good family, a Harvard man, a slightly overweight lawyer, with the face of a frustrated cherub—hardly, it would seem, an incendiary.

Rhode Island had always been the home of the contrary-minded. Rhode Islanders are contentious, cantankerous. Ever since the days of Anne Hutchinson and Roger Williams, who settled there because they could not get along with folks anywhere else, Rhode Islanders have been determinedly different. They tolerated Quakers, who didn't always tolerate one another: Nathanael Greene, the greatest fighting general of the Revolution, a belligerent blacksmith, had been read out of the Rhode Island meeting because of his military activities. They tolerated Jews—the oldest synagogue in America still stands in Newport—when Jews elsewhere were regarded as dangerous aliens, outcasts, *hostis humani generis*. They even put up with Baptists. It was only when they had exhausted all the objects of their broadmindedness that the Rhode Islanders started to fight among themselves, as they did in 1841, right after John Tyler had taken office.

The original thirteen colonies had been variously governed. Two, Connecticut and Rhode Island, operated under charters that were the envy of all the others. Connecticut's had been granted first, in 1662, when, it would seem, Charles II was in a generous mood. Fifteen months later this same monarch, in an even more generous mood, granted an even more liberal charter to the provincial agent from Rhode Island, and this was gleefully accepted by the Assembly of the Freemen of the Colony of Providence Plantations forgathered at Newport and presided over by Benedict Arnold (great-grandfather of the traitor).

Connecticut and Rhode Island were the only colonies that could elect their own governers. Governors of the other colonies, most of them appointed by the Crown, could send to London for royal review—disallowance—of any legislation they didn't like. The only way to keep these English governors in line, the colonies had learned, was by withholding their salaries, or threatening to. Most governors had paid heavily for their appointments and, in debt, looked upon the job as a means of establishing a fortune. Naturally they quaked when provincial legislators tugged at the public purse strings. When the ministers in London, together with the king, prepared to offset this coercion by arranging to pay the governors from the imperial treasury, they did more than any other one thing to bring about the Revolution.

Rhode Island and Connecticut, though immune to all

this, nevertheless joined the others when the war started.

Rhode Island's charter authorized a governor, a deputy governor, ten assistants, a General Assembly of Freemen consisting of seventy-two delegates, including four each from Providence, Portsmouth, Warwick, and six from Newport, then the largest town in the colony. This legislature was everything. The governor could negate its acts, but his veto could be overridden by a simple majority. As to the judiciary, Rhode Island judges were appointed by the assembly, to hold office for only a year at a time, and could be dismissed at any time for almost any reason.

All of this was fair enough. The difficulty came with the suffrage.

The men who had brought about the Revolution were not admirers of democracy as we define democracy today. They believed in rule by the competent, the well endowed, and when at last independence had been achieved and the colonies one by one adopted constitutions accordingly, they were rather stricter than they had previously been in the matter of eligibity to vote. These limitations were relaxed soon afterward, as Americans learned that no engulfment by an unlettered mob loomed; and as new states came into the union in the West, they did so with constitutions that called for open suffrage qualifications.

Rhode Island, founded as a community of radical ideals, in this matter alone proved conservative. Instead of lowering its suffrage requirements, it raised them.

Rhode Island was the only state that did not adopt a constitution. Its charter had worked all right for more than one hundred years, Rhode Islanders argued, so why change it?

The property qualification set by the Rhode Island assembly in earliest colonial times had been £100. This was doubled in 1729, doubled again in 1746 to £400, but in 1760 was cut to £40, as money values shifted. As an independent state, still under the royal charter, the assembly changed this into American money, setting it at $134, which was not remarkably high or low, as such things went then. But it stayed there, at $134 of land value, while requirements in the other states went down and down, soon to be eliminated.

In the old days such laws made little difference. Virtually everybody lived in the country, where there was plenty of land, so that a farmer could give his sons parcels of the same as they reached twenty-one, making them voters. But Rhode Island is a very small state, the smallest then as now, and its farm-voting acreage was soon used up. Moreover, the towns grew as artisans of various kinds, nonlandholders all, moved in. Representation became even more lopsided, and the "landocracy" had no intention of doing anything about it. There were squawks, of course, as there would have been even in a less contumacious place than Rhode Island. But the "Freemen," as they called themselves, ignored these. In 1840, when John Tyler was elected Vice President, sixteen of the thirty-one towns had a total population of 22,995 and sent to the assembly thirty-four representatives, whereas the 23,172 inhabitants of Providence were represented by only four. An assemblyman from Jamestown stood for 182 persons, one from Barrington for 274 persons, and one from Smithfield had a constituency of 4,757. The protests quite naturally increased, and it was at this time that Thomas Dorr came to the top as a leader, if at first a somewhat wan one.

Dorr was a Democrat, but in the early days of the

insurrection that was named after him, this made little difference. The Democrats floated at an all-time low in Rhode Island then. In 1841 the party even failed to nominate candidates for governor or for Congress. Nevertheless, every effort was made by the protesters to keep a bipartisan sheen on their cause. Thus, the president of the Woonsocket Suffrage Association was a Democrat, whereas the secretary was a Whig, and other groups followed this precedent. They were called the Suffrage party or the Friends of Suffrage, more often just Suffragists. As petitions for reform did no good—they could only be addressed to the assembly, which tabled them with hardly a glance—they began to organize parades, to display weapons, and to tamper with the militia.

The militia was made up of many scattered companies, not a few of which were "cadets" of one sort or another—that is, they considered themselves elite corps. Volunteer outfits, with their flamboyant, highly impractical uniforms and their menacing names—Eagle Guards, Jasper Greens, Avengers—they seemed somehow to foretell our present-day motorcycle gangs, and they were just about as reliable. Like all other units of the militia, they were answerable only to the governor. But—who *was* the governor of Rhode Island?

The Charter party had held a regular, restricted convention and named Samuel Ward King as governor. The Suffragists ceased to stage rallies that passed fiery resolutions and took direct action by holding their own convention, adopting their own constitution, and naming as governor Thomas Wilson Dorr.

Dorr received by far the larger vote—that was certain. But was this vote legal? His candidacy was favored by a majority of the men of Rhode Island—that was beyond doubt. But would those men fight for him? And even if they did—and even if they won—would the ensuing government be recognized by the United States?

The plight of Rhode Island was almost unbelievably complicated. King and Dorr had both prepared inaugural speeches. Something had to snap.

At this stage the two governors appealed to the President.

Here was the moment that everybody had feared. What would His Accidency do? His views about the sovereignty of the states were known, but there was no secret, either, about his fear of a national division. This Rhode Island business was swinging perilously close to a Democrat-Whig confrontation, with the Democrats backing Dorr, the Whigs' King. Should the federal government intervene? *Could* it?

Nothing like this had ever happened before. Daniel Shays's brushfire of 1786–87 had been a local affair, confined to a small part of western Massachusetts, and it occurred before the Constitution was adopted, before there was a real central government. The Whiskey Rebellion of 1794 was opposed by that archnationalist Alexander Hamilton, but he and his army arrived on the scene only after the unfortunate local misunderstanding had been straightened out; moreover, the Whiskey Rebellion had been caused by resistance to a federal tax law and was not a matter of states' rights. Consequently, the constitutional right of the federal government to meddle with—or intervene in or adjudicate—the internal squabbles of a sovereign state had never been decided.

The Rhode Islanders never denied the supremacy of the central government in Washington. But their internal quarrel was the sort of thing that could explode, causing an unconfinable fire. Connecticut, Massachusetts, and New York were taking an ominous interest in the Rhode Island doings. The air was filled with fitful threats.

Governor King made the first appeal. He wrote two letters to the President, the first formal, the second less so, both urgent, begging the government "to suppress such insurrectionary and lawless assemblies . . . and . . . protect the State from domestic violence." He sent these to Washington by three trusted friends, rich businessmen, who were received at the White House.

The President then wrote and entrusted to his visitors one answer. He was grave. He had been asked "questions of municipal regulation," he wrote, "with which this Government can have nothing to do." However, while staving off an incipient revolt would be unconstitutional, if such a revolt *was* started, Washington could be counted upon to do its duty by assuring Rhode Island of a stable republican government, as required by the Constitution.

In other words, come back when you've got an honest-to-goodness revolution.

Much was made of this letter, which the Charter Whigs hailed as a promise of military assistance, whereas the Democrats in general denounced it as a threat of federal interference in state affairs.

Now Dorr spoke up. He had quit Providence stealthily and in haste, some said because he feared arrest. He was known to have been in New York for a little while, conferring no doubt with friends who were members of the Society of Saint Tammany. *They* urged him to take his case to the President of the United States. He did so. At least, he went to Washington. He might or might not have been received at the White House, and if he was, or even if he wasn't, no doubt he was informed of John Tyler's "benign neutrality" stand; no doubt, too, he interpreted this as an out-and-out endorsement of the Charterists' cause. There is no official record.

Back in New York, Thomas Wilson Dorr again was made much of by the sachems of Saint Tammany, who pledged him all sorts of support. Tammany had started as a veterans' society just after the Revolution, originally nonpolitical and harmless enough, even rather childish with its Indian suits and feathers and titles, fond of parading. By 1842 it had become a powerful influence in politics, its "braves" the Bowery Boys and suchlike gangsters, hooligans. These ruffians were rallied in large numbers to cheer for Governor Dorr and to pledge him support in his fight against "the landocracy," tyranny, special privileges. Dorr seems to have been impressed. Volunteer military outfits marched before him. He was presented with a sword that had been carried by a now dead young lieutenant in the Second Seminole War, just finished. He was presented with copies of all sorts of high-sounding resolutions. When after several days of cheers and applause he was prepared to take a boat to Stonington, Connecticut, he was escorted to the dock by a troop of cavalry, and Levi D. Slamm, the persuasive editor of the *New Era,* promised him a thousand "fighting men" anytime he blew the whistle.

He arrived at Stonington Sunday morning, May 15, and took a train to Providence the next morning. In Providence he was met by a crowd of some three thousand, perhaps a tenth of them armed. He stood in his carriage and made them a long speech to the effect that the time for speeches was past. Previously he had been meek, if insistent, but now he was full of fight. He drew the Seminole

War sword and waved it above his head, shouting that it had been bloodied once in the defense of their beloved country and could be bloodied again, here, unless they got their rights. (In fact that sword never had known gore. The young lieutenant who carried it succumbed to dysentery in Florida before he had a chance to meet the foe, but Thomas Dorr probably didn't know this, and certainly the crowd didn't.)

There are various accounts of this speech, but all are agreed that it called for action, action. Sheriff Potter, who was a part of the crowd, had in his pocket a warrant for the arrest of "Governor" Dorr, but he decided not to try to serve it at that time.

The followers of Dorr, a notably undisciplined pack, stole two cannons from a militia post. These were guns left over from the Revolution, though it was believed that both were operable. The Dorrites loaded them and hauled them off to their headquarters, Burrington Anthony's house facing down Atwell Avenue. That night—it was May 17 and foggy—Dorr used them in a threat to the arsenal on Cranston Road. This was a strong stone building of two stories, and it was filled with militiamen of proved orthodoxy, armed, in uniform, and responsive to command. They might have numbered two hundred. About the same number approached the place from the northeast, hauling those two stout cannons. Dorr, as governor, formally called upon the garrison of the arsenal to surrender, and he was answered by the commanding officer there, who said that he knew of no Governor Dorr.

It was an impossible position. Even if the cannons could be made to fire—they had been out in the fog for many hours—they could not be reloaded, for there was no more powder, no more ball. The arsenal, uphill of Dorr's men, could hardly get damaged. With the dawn, and visibility, its garrison could charge.

Nevertheless Thomas Dorr ordered that the cannons be fired. Again, accounts differ. Some have it that Dorr applied the linstock in person, some do not, but they all agree, at least, that he gave the order.

The priming on the first cannon flared stodgily, but it did not ignite the powder at the touchhole, which was undoubtedly damp. There was the equivalent of a flash in the pan. With the second cannon it was the same.

Discouraged, more and more of Dorr's men slipped away into the fog, and when dawn did smear the sky, reluctantly, he had fewer than fifty left. He fled, abandoning the cannons. Pursued by sundry "cadet" outfits, who themselves got lost in what was left of the fog, he made for Woonsocket, eventually to get back to New York, where he downed another heady draft of overconfidence administered by the sons of Saint Tammany.

Shots had been fired, or almost fired. Governor Samuel Ward King wrote again to John Tyler, his third letter.

The President had already alerted the commanding officers of all army posts in New England, asking for reports, and now he consulted with Daniel Webster, the only New Englander in his Cabinet. They framed a Presidential proclamation, declaring that

> Whereas the legislature of the State of Rhode Island has applied to the President of the United States, setting forth the existence of a dangerous insurrection in that State, composed partly of deluded citizens of the State, but chiefly of intruders of dangerous and abandoned character coming from other States, and requiring the immediate interposition of the constitutional power vested in him to be

> exercised in such cases, I do issue this my proclamation, according to law, hereby commanding all insurgents, and all persons connected with the said insurrection, to disperse and retire peaceably to their respective abodes within twenty-four hours from the time when this proclamation shall be made public in Rhode Island.

This paper was never posted. It was not dated, not signed by the President or countersigned by the Secretary of State. It remains in this form in the archives today.

The President had agreed to send a friend of Daniel Webster to study the situation on Rhode Island, and this person, who served anonymously, was about to bring in a report. Before he could do so, Thomas Wilson Dorr had lost his head entirely. Leaving New York Tuesday, June 21, he arrived in Norwich, Connecticut, on the steamboat *New Haven* early the next morning, and from there, with a handful of men, he marched to Chepachet, Rhode Island, where he made an attempt to fortify Acote's Hill, an eighty-foot elevation near the center of the village. It was a poor place, for it was commanded by a higher spot nearby, where the militia's artillerymen, who were reported to be near, could mount several guns. It was, however, close to both the Massachusetts and Connecticut lines.

Acote's Hill was charged by a large force of militiamen with fixed bayonets at 7:45 A.M., Tuesday, June 28. Nobody was killed, because nobody was there. Thomas Wilson Dorr and his highly unreliable army had disappeared into the surrounding countryside.

The only casualties of the whole "war" occurred the next day, when militiamen, striving to stop the escape of Dorrites over the Seekonk River bridge at Pawtucket, shot three persons on the Massachusetts side, killing one. All three were innocent bystanders.

Governor King, who had just written a fourth letter to the President, a letter John Tyler did not answer, now declared martial law. Hundreds were jailed. Dorr returned from Connecticut voluntarily, and was imprisoned. He conducted his own defense at his trial for treason, that defense being chiefly that a citizen could not commit treason against a state, only against the national government. Dorr was dignified, himself again. He was found guilty and sentenced to hard labor for life. All of the other prisoners were eventually released.

Martial law was suspended August 8, 1842. In April of the following year there was an election in which 16,520 voted for governor, nearly twice as many as ever before. A convention was called, a new constitution adopted, and Charles II's charter ceased to operate May 2. The Dorrites, though Dorr himself was still in jail, won most of their claims. The suffrage was liberalized.

Thomas Wilson Dorr, no rabble-rouser, not a popular public figure, took his punishment without whimpering, but his friends, and even many who had been opposed to his suffrage movement, were shocked by the life sentence, and from the very beginning there had been pressure on the governor to pardon him. This the governor did. Dorr spent exactly one year in prison. He was shaken, a changed man, much older, and he died a few years later.

Men who make war, *if* they win, often are heaped with medals, titles, scrolls containing words of praise. It is not so with men who make peace. The Dorr War had its comic-opera aspects, true, but it was a real threat to the continuance of the American union. Asked what he did during that crisis, John Tyler might have replied, like the French cleric who was asked what he did in the French Revolution, "I survived." In fact Tyler did much more than that. He might well have saved his country.

9

★ ★ ★

The Menace of the North

There was also the Second Seminole War, which unlike the first was expensive and noteworthy for heroics, indeed in some of its aspects downright embarrassing; but this had been quieted—and lost—before John Tyler took over at the White House. The Texas war too was finished, although Mexico wouldn't admit this, and another eruption down there might be expected at any time. The Aroostook War in Maine, largely a lumberjacks' affair, simmered at the back of the stove. The really big scare was Canada.

Canada was boiling over, a geyser, spouting sulfurous steam.

Canada, it must be understood, was not one place, not one government, but seven. There was Newfoundland—rocky, chill, remote. There were the Maritimes—Nova Scotia, New Brunswick, Prince Edward Island. There was Lower Canada, Quebec; and Upper Canada, which was Ontario. Each of these had its own royal governor. There was also the vast frozen Hudson's Bay country, run like a private fief by the Hudson's Bay Company. It was this company and its furring activities, its claims to the land along the Columbia River, that especially concerned those who backed the Astor interests in that part of the world and who would have had the United States take over the entire Oregon country, clear up to 54 degrees 40 minutes north latitude (to include the present Queen Charlotte Islands). But it was Lower Canada and Upper Canada that the average American meant when he named this land, and it was there that the trouble started.

It was meant to be—it announced itself as—a war for independence. As such it should have been an internal business that would not concern those on the United States side of the border, but sympathy with the rebels was keen among those who lived in upper New York State, upper New Hampshire, Maine, Vermont; and insurgents who escaped across the line were given help when they planned to return to Canada. These returns often took the form of barn-burning raids, and after the raiders had done their damage, it was easy for them to slip back under the protection of the United States. Then the governor of Upper Canada or the governor of Lower Canada would write to the President of the United States, demanding that the fugitives be returned, and the President of the United States, whether John Tyler or his predecessor Martin Van Buren, would reply by pointing out that he had no jurisdiction, that it would be necessary to apply to the governor of the state involved, something that was always hard to explain to any British official.

"Imitation is the sincerest flattery." Yankees of the 1830–40's (it might be harder for those of today) could see many similarities between the glorious American Revolution and these sudden, furious, Canadian flare-ups, and naturally the sympathy of many of them, especially those who lived near the border, was with the underdog. Hatred of kings, too, still was hot in those days, when anything English was worth a curse. Also, the despised American Tories had flown in large numbers to Canada and settled there; and these of course were now, as they had been before, on the side of the Crown.

The Yankees professed to see some likeness to Samuel Adams, if a Samuel Adams with a French accent, in Louis-Joseph Papineau, speaker of the Quebec assembly and the chief complainer in Lower Canada, as they professed also to see a similarity between John Wilkes and William Lyon Mackenzie, Upper Canada's leading firebrand. Each of these two provinces had issued its own Declaration of Independence. In each, liberty poles were erected in public places, and some of these were surmounted with bright-red Phrygian caps, while high-sounding resolutions were adopted at noisy rallies. There was even a confrontation between the embattled farmers and the redcoats at Saint-Denis and at Saint-Charles on the Richelieu River, and some men sentimentally compared this with Lexington-Concord, although in the Canadian case the farmers did not fight back but dispersed sheepishly at the first command.

The Yankees, from earliest times, had suffered under the illusion that Canada, the *real people* of Canada, had always been eager to become a part of the United States—and this despite the fact that no fewer than five invasions, three in the Revolution, two during the War of 1812, had been ignominiously driven back. The Canadians "were us," really, the Yankees fondly supposed, and given half a chance would gladly fly into our arms.

That our northern neighbors might not want to be liberated, at least not in the manner indicated by us, seems never to have occurred to the Yankees of New England and New York, who flocked with guns and money to the various exiles' groups—the Canadian Refugee Relief Association, the Sons of Liberty, the Patriots, the Hunters' Lodges *(Frères Chasseurs),* and Canada Liberation—and often accompanied raiding parties into the land to the north.

Great Britain protested; and the Foreign Minister of Great Britain at this time happened to be Lord Palmerston, a bellicose fop, "half hornet and half butterfly"—in the office they called him Lord Pumicestone—who believed in gunboat diplomacy and was inclined to answer any question with a straight right to the jaw. Palmerston did nothing to still the troubled waters.

Following the rule that usually governs such an occasion, each side accused the other of provocation, while itself making preparations for conflict. When the trouble started, late in November of 1837, Great Britain had almost no troops stationed in the Canadas. The U.S. Army then had a paper strength of 7,958, although it did not actually number much over 5,000, and nine of the thirteen regular regiments, including all of the artillery, were far down in the Everglades floundering around in an effort to find the pesky Seminoles. By the time John Tyler came into power, Britain had 5,000 regular troops in the Canadas, where the garrisons at Halifax and Quebec had been strengthened and a new fort had been built at Kingston. The U.S. Army, pulling troops back from Florida, had rebuilt military posts at Sackett's Harbor, Oswego, and Niagara, all on or near the border, and erected a new one at Ogdensburg. On September 4, 1841, Congress passed a special appropriation bill providing well over $2 million, and $50,000 of this went for a new barracks and defensive works at Buffalo, $75,000 more for a fort at the northern end of Lake Champlain, $100,000 for a couple of armed steamers on Lake Erie. The last item is significant. Despite the Rush-Bagot agreement for naval disarmament on the Great Lakes, an agreement made after the War of 1812, the British too were reported to have laid plans and appropriated money for armed steamers. All of this, of course, was done in the name of defense. It is always the other fellow who starts the fight.

The matter was further complicated by the fact that large numbers on both sides, while avowing their love of peace, *wanted* war. Civil war, the bitterest, nastiest kind, the Canadians already had, but they sought to promote a war between Great Britain and the United States. The Patriots, the Canadian Liberationists, believed that only by means of such a conflict could they gain a major ally, just as the struggling colonies to the south of them had striven to get France into *their* fight, saving them. As for the zealots south of the border, they saw that assisting the exiles would not be enough, and despite repeated proofs to the contrary they clung to a fond belief that the whole of the great northern land was ripe, now as always, for the picking. Thus, the War Hawks quite frankly coveted all of Canada, which they were confident they could conquer. Under Tyler, John S. Chipman was to tell the House of Representatives that "Michigan alone would take Canada in ninety days."

All of this greatly troubled the new President. Before he

could take steps to annex Texas, he knew that he must settle the Canadian threat, which seemed to grow louder with every passing day. A recently created peer, Lord Ashburton, head of the banking house of Baring, was preparing to visit the United States as a special ambassador for the purpose of ironing out the American-Canadian boundary dispute with the Secretary of State in Washington, and the rumble in the north could well cause these negotiations to be called off.

John Tyler issued a proclamation declaring that the United States intended to respect all neutrality laws, and in addition he warned his fellow countrymen against giving unauthorized material assistance to Canadian rebels, for if they were caught in Canada with arms in their hands, he said, their country would not go to their assistance.

A mild-mannered Scot, Lord Aberdeen, came to the Foreign Office, replacing the fire-snorting Palmerston, and the banker-diplomat Ashburton did visit the United States after all, although he did so in the manner of a man who takes his life in his hands. Ashburton and Daniel Webster got along famously from the very beginning, Ashburton being amazed to find that there were some gentlemen in the United States. They held many man-to-man meetings in Black Dan's office, leaving no official record, making no reports. President Tyler sometimes sat in on these sessions, and always he kept in touch with their progress, holding himself in readiness to give advice at any time.

The Webster-Ashburton talks were of interest to the President for yet another reason. Black Dan was the only New Englander in his Cabinet, almost the only Northerner. He was the one Secretary who had failed to resign on orders from Henry Clay. His excuse for remaining for a time in the Cabinet of an excommunicated Whig, an ex-Democrat, was exactly this prolonged discussion with the British ambassador, a long while looming. Tyler might have questioned this, in his secret mind. Without being unduly cynical, he might have thought, as Clay did, and many another, that Webster too had the Presidential bee in his bonnet. The Archangel was notoriously a glory grabber, and it was being predicted in Washington that if the Ashburton talks were a success, he would take all the curtain calls himself.

As Webster had fooled Lord Ashburton, so he fooled the Washingtonians by sharing with John Tyler the credit for these famous talks. The President, he handsomely said, had been a great help. Ashburton himself confirmed this.

Meanwhile the whole business was almost blown to pieces and the country plunged into war by an eructation of the *Caroline* case.

She was a small cargo vessel, privately owned, based at Buffalo, and she had been extensively used to haul supplies to Navy Island, an uninhabited spot huddled against the north bank of the Niagara River. Navy Island was Canadian property—Upper Canada—and it was being used as an advance base by William Lyon Mackenzie, who was preparing, quite openly, an attack upon Toronto. Hence, when *Caroline* was going about her routine duties at port or on the open lake, she could be considered a neutral vessel, but while she was tied up at Navy Island, she was unquestionably breaking the law, her cargo subject to confiscation, her crew to arrest.

Caroline was supposed to be at Navy Island the night of December 29, 1837, and it was there that a party of militiamen from Upper Canada sought her out. They were late. She had left, having returned to Buffalo, where, presumably, the crew would celebrate another successful gunrunning. The militiamen seized whatever supplies and arms they could find, but it was the *Caroline* herself that they had really set out for, so they pushed across the river and boarded the offending craft. There was a scuffle, a shot, and one man fell, badly wounded. He was a sailor called Durfree, a United States citizen.

The militiamen chased the other sailors ashore, stripped the *Caroline* of everything that might possibly be called contraband, set her on fire, and pushed her out into the river. This happened within sound of the famous falls, toward which *Caroline* started to drift. She never got there. A mass of flames, she went under.

Meanwhile Durfree had died.

Here, clearly, was a case for the State Department, not just the governor of New York, and the State Department responded with a prompt and emphatic protest, demanding an apology and reparations. Lord Palmerston was still in office, and they got neither. Another protest was sent, and another. There was no satisfactory acknowledgment of these. The British position was that the *Caroline* attack had been a measure of defense and made in "hot pursuit." State persisted. The nation seethed. Palmerston sneered.

There was in Upper Canada a deputy sheriff named Alexander McLeod, of Niagara County, and he was often sent to the United States to demand the return of fugitives, errands that made him unpopular in that part of New York State. McLeod had been a member of the *Caroline* raiding party, and one night when drinking, he had been heard to boast that he was the one who shot Durfree. He was arrested in New York twice while engaged in pursuing his duty, and each time the Canadian authorities got him back by sending a cash bail. The third time, November 12, 1840, it was different. He was arrested on a charge of murder, at Lewiston, New York, and taken to Lockport, Lewiston having no jail. Canada offered to supply bail and sent deputy sheriffs to get the man back, but a mob surrounded the jail, declaring that McLeod must stand trial. The Canadians withdrew.

Now it was Whitehall's turn to protest—noisily, vehemently. The State Department replied that it had no jurisdiction, that this matter was up to the governor of New York. So Whitehall protested to the governor of New York, who replied coldly that McLeod would have to stand trial.

The governor was the same William H. Seward who a little while before had decided, in company with the taciturn Thurlow Weed, to wrest power from the Albany Regency, placing it firmly in the hands of the Whigs. He had succeeded in this, but he was not sure enough of his position to risk such an unpopular move as the release of Alexander McLeod. Or perhaps Seward, a man who had his own eye on the White House, really believed that McLeod would get a fair trial. The British Foreign Office clearly did not believe this. They called the mob at the Lockport jail a lynch mob. They cried that McLeod was as good as dead if he was not immediately returned to Canada.

The angry men in London appealed once again to Washington. Tyler and his Secretary of State Webster both were known to be eager to keep Whitehall's good faith, but they firmly, if apologetically, declined to interfere. The most that they would do was assure Governor Seward of their willingness to cooperate in any way, and assign a lawyer from the Attorney General's office to help McLeod frame his defense.

Canada never had known a frontier like that of the United States, and it didn't want one. In London the Foreign Office men simply took it for granted that Alexander McLeod, no matter what his defense, would be found guilty of murder and hanged. They believed that lynch law was the only law of the American West, and were determined to protect their own nationals against it. The best way to do this, they thought, was by screaming threats of war.

They believed implicitly the story of the Yankee frontiersman who denied that anybody ever was lynched in that part of the world. "We always give 'em a fair trial before we hang 'em," he said.

Palmerston had gone, Aberdeen was in command, and the Webster-Ashburton talks came to a comfortable conclusion, but peace seemed farther away than ever. The issue was heated almost to the bursting point when Alexander McLeod was brought to trial in New York State. "This means *war!*" screamed the British press. They called the treaty Ashburton's Capitulation. They demanded that more troops be sent to Canada.

The evidence against McLeod was extremely weak, hearsay. He was acquitted.

There would be no war.

10

★ ★ ★

Preparing to Pair with a Prickly Pear

How to tackle Texas? That was the question. When a girl has taken advantage of the year divisible by four and has proposed marriage to the gentleman of her choice and has been turned down, she would be somewhat less than human if she did not wax wary of this same swain when next he came calling. And this had happened to the proud new republic of Texas *four times*.

Four times she had been left, as she herself was pleased to put it, waiting at the church. No reasonable explanation for this conduct ever was vouchsafed by the masterminds at Washington.

In the beginning there had been no doubt of the Texan desire to become a part of the United States of America. The new republic's constitution had been modeled after the one adopted in 1787 at Philadelphia, and in a plebiscite in September of 1836 it had voted overwhelmingly in favor of annexation. In December of that same year it had formally offered itself to the United States, through its minister in Washington. The request was never properly answered, and in 1837 Texas, unabashed, tried again. Will you marry me? she had asked. Once more, no reply; and the Lone Star Republic, after waiting an unconscionable time, had withdrawn the suggestion.

People don't like to be treated that way; and neither do governments.

The President of Texas was Sam Houston, the victor at San Jacinto, a protégé of the arch-annexationist Andrew Jackson. Houston was gruff, tough, monosyllabic—although he did name one of his daughters Patience Elizabeth Texas Louisiana—but his annexation ardor was damped, to say the least of it, by this double rebuff. His successor, Mirabeau Buonaparte Lamar, who wrote poetry, never had favored a melding with the states of the effete East. Lamar thought that Texas, remaining independent, should expand itself by taking in large chunks of northern Mexican territory, and he made an expensive try at this, causing a needy republic to become even needier.

(Texas, it should be pointed out, had no immediate available cash assets, was some $7.5 million in debt, and was issuing paper money that brought only 12 cents on the dollar.)

Houston and Lamar aside, there was an exceptionally large knot of New Englanders among the creators of Texas—Memucan Hunt, Bernard E. Bee, Anson Jones, Ebenezer Allen, Ashbel Smith, and of course the Austins themselves, father and son. Most of the settlers, however, had come from Missouri, Tennessee, Arkansas, Louisiana, Mississippi. They were not likely to change their sentimental allegiance to the home territory any more than they might change their ideas about the ownership of slaves.

It must not be thought that at any time John Tyler or any member of his "corporal's guard" of followers in Congress—Henry Clay himself had bestowed that name upon them—were working merely for *annexation* of Texas. No, no! What they sought, rather, what they insisted upon, was *re*annexation. This claim had a murky background. It was based, in the first place, on the assumption that the current republic of Texas had once been—geographically if not politically—a part of the French–Spanish–French territory of Louisiana, and that as such it had been sold to the United States under Thomas Jefferson in the biggest real-estate deal in history. Nobody could prove this claim, but neither could anybody with any authority disprove it. The Louisiana Purchase never had been exactly defined. Its eastern boundary was clear—the Mississippi River. Its southern boundary was equally obvious—the Gulf of Mexico. But how far north did it go? and how far west? In the absence of maps, or surveys, nobody knew. There were some who professed to believe that it extended clear to the Pacific Ocean, embracing, of course, all of California, all of what was then loosely known as New Mexico and today is New Mexico, Arizona, Utah, Nevada, Montana, perhaps part of Idaho. The Tyler forces did not go that far, but they did contend that the Purchase at least included all of Texas, its southern and western boundaries being the Rio Grande, no less. Hence we were not plotting to take over part of a neighbor's inheritance but only to repossess what had always been rightfully ours. *Re*annexation, then, not just annexation.

The word was a rallying cry.

True, when the United States had purchased the Floridas from Spain, which at that time was in undisputed possession of Mexico, there was a stipulation in the treaty that United States claims should not go west of the Sabine River, and this stream too had been accepted by mutual agreement in the field between Spanish and American forces at the time when General James Wilkinson thought that he needed all his men for the protection of New Orleans from the south-coming rag-tag-and-bobtail forces headed by Aaron Burr; but these objections the *re*annexationists waved away. They had a very good thing in that prefix, and they meant to use it to the full.

Unfortunately they could not block its appropriation by the Fifty-Four-Forty-or-Fight people. Oregon too was a vast region with unclear limits. Great Britain and the United States on several occasions had failed to agree upon a line between their claims, and the claims themselves, in any case, were of a differing nature. The Hudson's Bay Company, frowning down from the north, wanted to keep Oregon a skimpily settled land, out of which industrious Indians could fetch many pelts, while the Americans who were beginning to crowd in from the east wanted a well-settled land, a land devoted to agriculture. Many of these Americans were missionaries. All of them thought that their cause was being ignored by the federal government at Washington, and they seized eagerly upon that useful prefix "re" and began to talk about and write about and insist upon the *re*annexation or the *re*occupation of Oregon. They had no more justification for this than the Tylerites had for their "re" claim, but who cared? The Tylerites, thinking, naturally, of 1844, used the occasion to concoct some more alliterative campaign slogans: Tyler and Texas! and No Texas, No Oregon! It might be called a standoff.

It is remarkable that at this time there entered into all discussions of American expansionism—Manifest Destiny, it was coming to be called, though the irreverent preferred the Great Land Grab—that powerful argument, the Biblical citation. If you could quote the Bible about it, then it was all right. The Oregon missionaries were in large part responsible for this effort to give the whole greedy movement an orthodox Christian glow, although the quotation they most relied upon was distinctly pre-Christian: "And God blessed them, and God said to them, 'Be fruitful and multiply, and replenish the earth, and subdue it.' " (Genesis 1:28.) The Hudson's Bay people, the missionaries complained, were not doing anything to *exploit* the great territory of Oregon; they were not even trying to make it fruitful and to populate it; and hence they should not be granted dominion over it.

One bright afternoon in May, President Tyler was visited by a strange and rather fierce figure on horseback, who left his steed at the front door and strode purposefully into the East Room, where the Secretary of State, Daniel Webster, just happened to be. This was the Reverend Dr. Marcus Whitman, a missionary from the West Coast, who had ridden four thousand miles—or so he said, and he said it repeatedly—in order to tell Mr. Tyler something about the territory of Oregon. A large crowd of church people waited outside, with the horse. This visit was supposed to be impromptu, a spur-of-the-moment thing, but in truth it had been well prepared and probably even rehearsed.

It must have been a curious scene. Dr. Whitman, clad in boot moccasins, buckskin breeches, fur leggings, a buffalo overcoat with head hood thrown back, showed in his face and hands that he had been through a great deal of unpleasant weather. Excited, he never sat down, but strode the East Room floor, windmilling his arms. The two statesmen regarded him gravely, nodding as he made his points. He was a man of medium height, with thick shoulders, a large head, stiff iron-gray hair and beard, a shaggy man, a snorter. He talked for two hours, with many gestures.

There is no record of this lecture; but doubtless the battered man of God told about how at the behest of the American Board of Foreign Missions he and his girl-bride Narcissa, the first white woman to cross the Rockies, in the company of sundry others had trudged from Independence, Missouri, over the Snake River route into Oregon; about the stunning beauty of that land, and its fertility; about the threat from the north, the far side of the great Columbia River, where Englishmen were working to take over this earthly paradise; and about how he and certain of his friends and associates had agreed that the Board of Foreign Missions in Boston should be notified—and also the Great White Father in Washington.

No doubt Dr. Whitman recited a tale already familiar to his well-informed audience when he described how a Yankee skipper, Robert Gray, discovered the mouth of the Columbia—until that time a west-flowing river of myth; how Captains Meriwether Lewis and William Clark, of the U.S. Army, had examined and mapped the approaches to this river from the east, and the coast adjacent to its mouth; how John Jacob Astor in search of furs had established the first white settlement in that part of the world, and how this had been seized by the Royal Navy in the War of 1812; how the two nations in 1818 decided that they couldn't decide on a boundary and postponed this for ten years, to 1828, when they decided the same thing again, leaving the matter wide open; how, recently, according to reports, the diplomatic bigwigs here in Washington had agreed with their opposite numbers from London to do the same thing yet again—that is, to postpone any understanding as to what and where Oregon in fact was, settling instead for a minor rearrangement of the international line through Maine and Quebec and the Lakes region.

Here Black Dan must have bowed his head. No one knew better than he that the Ashburton talks were about to come to an end without having established any boundary farther west than Minnesota. But he was not about to interrupt a representative of the ABFM.

Dr. Whitman was emphatic, and probably very loud, as though he hoped that his words might reach the parishioners who hovered outside. He painted a glowing picture of the Oregon territory, at great length. Afterward each of the statesmen thanked him, shaking his hand, and John Tyler, always courteous, accompanied him to the door.

Much was made of this interview in the public prints and in the barrooms of the land. It is unlikely that government policy was in any way altered by it, but it did inaugurate and set the pattern for a long series of White House publicity stunts.

What Oregon meant to John Tyler, even after Dr. Whitman's detailed description, was a balance to the annexation of Texas, a balance that was doing his cause no good. There was no connection between the two issues, and in the matter of the extension of slavery they were at odds. This was demonstrated by the behavior of John Quincy Adams, the curmudgeon, who had given up all hope of getting back into the White House but who was still a power in American politics, a mover and doer in the House of Representatives. It was the ex-President who had quashed the second Texan request for membership, in the spring of 1838, when he talked it to death in the House, one of the first successful filibusters. Again, in March of 1843, J. Q. Adams, together with twelve other members of the House, issued to the American people a circular that urged them *not* "to receive into their family and fraternity such misbegotten and illegitimate progeny" as Texas. It was a vitriolic document, this circular, in many ways extraordinary, certainly without precedent, and it darkly warned that annexation, or even *re*annexation, "would be identical with dissolution." Against such thundering did John Tyler strive.

The first two Texas entrance tries had been made before His Accidency came into power. With the third and fourth he was immediately connected.

Webster had resigned from State May 8, 1843, and this made a considerable difference in the reannexation program. Webster came from Massachusetts, where the abolition forces were growing at an alarming rate, and anyway he was known to be against the annexation of Texas. Now the conferences with Ashburton were finished, and he was glad to be able to step out of a Cabinet in which for some time he had been the only holdover. Like the President himself, he was thinking of the 1844 election, and each of them feared that continued political association with the other would hurt his chances. Webster, then, backed out with a begrudged bow, and Tyler was free to get a Secretary of State more sympathetic to the cause of the Lone Star Republic.

This was Abel P. Upshur of Virginia, who until this time had been Secretary of the Navy, and who was a close personal friend of His Accidency. Another Virginian, Thomas Walker Gilmer, was made Secretary of the Navy. This meant that Mr. Tyler's Cabinet, originally mixed, now was made up almost exclusively of Southerners, a significant fact and one much marked by the Democrats, whose good opinion he was eager to regain. Only John C. Spencer, the Secretary of War, came from a northern state, New York (and he and Upshur did not get on well together: once they almost broke up a Cabinet meeting when they started to swing at one another).

Now was the time, surely, for further action on the *re*annexation front; and this was promptly forthcoming.

Lamar the unpredictable was out, Sam Houston back in; and Houston decided, early in 1842, that Texas should knock for admission once again, now that he had a friend in the White House. He sent General Henderson to Washington with instructions to work toward this end with the Texan minister there, Isaac Van Zandt. It really looked, for a little while, as if the great addition at last was to be made.

Various things intervened to prevent this, one of them the loudest explosion the country ever had heard.

11

★ ★ ★

The Biggest Bang

Defense, in Tyler's time, used to be called war. Americans of those days had not yet been brought to a state of mind that would denominate a machine built to drop bombs upon a land four thousand miles away not as a killer but as an instrument of defense, while the men who controlled these devices were acting under the tutelage not of the War Department but of the Department of Defense. Americans were susceptible to semantic refinement in Tyler's time, but they had not yet reached the point where they could call every attack an act of self-protection. Perhaps they were naive.

The army had always been a suspect institution in the United States, where the militia system, although it had proved itself not even good for *defensive* defense purposes, was preferred. The aversion to a full-time professional army, some said, was a holdover from Commonwealth days in England, where Oliver Cromwell had shown how easy it was to crush a nation's liberty by military means, whatever the cause. The army in the United States had been occupied in dirty frontier work, holding back the redskins, teaching them new forms of terrorism. It was not a thing of decoration, a glittering assemblage on display in court or on the parade ground. If admired at all, it was admired only from a distance. Mostly it was feared, and there was a general agreement that it must be kept in hand.

The case of the navy was different. Americans were then a coastal people, a seagoing people, and admiration for the tarry-breeks or tar was loud among them. Somehow, although he stank, he seemed a *cleaner* man than the soldier. Also, the naval officers, if traditionally brutal, rude, abrupt, and not drawn from the upper classes, as were the army leaders of Europe, were putting on airs—dress swords, epaulettes, gold braid, bicornes—so that they could be quite as dazzling as any royal guardsmen.

Technically, the army still was the senior service, but the navy was catching up with it.

The big-navy men were aware that only the *biggest* navy counted. There was no second place in this early arms race, no consolation prize. Yet though the Royal Navy had a tremendous start, so that it seemed that no other nation could overtake it, the big-navy men in America went on calling for more ships, more guns and bigger ones, more men. They were fond of pointing to the supreme achievement of the Royal Navy in maintaining a blockade of France all through the Napoleonic wars. The fact that she could do this and still, with her left hand, as it were, chase the miserable little U.S. Navy up its rivers to shivering safety, to expensive inactivity, establishing a full-length blockade of the American coast at the same time—this fact did not seem to dismay the big-navy men. They insisted that if only this country's sea force were increased by, say, about fiftyfold, or a hundredfold, such a thing would not be likely to happen again. Where the money to pay for all this might come from they did not say.

It was at this time that a second great change came in the methods of modern naval warfare—the first having been, of course, that from Mediterranean to deep-sea tactics, from the long ship to the beamy, from oars to sail, from ramming to the broadside. This second great change was from wooden ships to iron, from sail to steam.

England had built up her enormous navy despite shortages. Her own stands of oak had long since proved insufficient, whereas those in the vast forests of America after the Revolution were no longer hers, and she had to get the timber with which her stout ships were built from Norway and Sweden, just as she had to get less heavy naval materials—cordage, tar, canvas—from the Baltic countries. But when the great change came, Great Britain had ample iron in her mines at home, ample coal with which to render this into steel. The United States had neither of these, and France not much.

John Tyler was not a big-navy enthusiast, no island-snatcher who favored the establishment of coaling stations all around the world so that the United States flag could be carried everywhere in the new steamships. But he definitely did approve of a larger, if not the largest, navy. Although always an earnest worker for peace, he often had a good word for the despised, dispersed U.S. Army, and privately and in public poohpoohed the suggestion, rife just then, that the officers' training academy at West Point be dismantled and disbanded as an unnecessary expense, an experiment that had failed. He was even heard to say a few words of approval for the wild idea of establishing a similar officers' training school for the navy—at, say, Annapolis, Maryland.

He was, indisputably, pro-navy. More, he was big-navy. It was the one respect in which he differed from his mentor Thomas Jefferson, the farmer, who thought that many shallow-water gunboats rather than a few deep-sea battle wagons could protect the long Atlantic coastline.

It was no more than natural, then, that when he was invited to inspect U.S.S. *Princeton* and to cruise in her along the lower Potomac, on February 22, 1844, John Tyler accepted with alacrity.

Princeton was a sloop-of-war, the pride of the Navy, a vessel spanking-new in a service sometimes accused of being bound by tradition, blind to progress.

Designed by John Ericsson, an engineering genius recently arrived from Sweden, she was the first warship in the world equipped with screw propellers, Ericsson's own invention. This was extremely important in naval warfare. Sidewheelers, with their huge paddle coping starboard and port, were vulnerable to cannon fire and could be crippled in a matter of seconds; but all of *Princeton's* propelling apparatus was below water, where balls could not reach it. More—and the Navy made a great thing of this—*Princeton* was the first war steamer in the world *all* of whose machinery was below the waterline, and so, like the propellers, not readily reached by gunfire.

She carried auxiliary sails, of course, but even without these she was supposed to be very fast and easy on coal, a fact of which the Navy made much. (When she had been thoroughly shaken down, shortly after this Potomac cruise, *Princeton* was to make it from Galveston, Texas, to Annapolis in nine days, using only ninety-three tons of fuel, a record.)

Here was no ordinary occasion. Aside from its interest to naval-engineering circles, the cruise was to be a landmark in Washington social history. Everybody who was anybody would be there, and it was only natural that the President himself should head the list. The host, it might be mentioned, the man who issued the invitations, was the skipper of this sensational new ship, Captain Robert F. ("Fighting Bob") Stockton, currently the head of a family of wealthy landowners. The Stocktons had interests in the Red River district of Arkansas, and also in Georgia, Virginia, and in far California, as well as in their own home district of Somerset County, New Jersey. Captain Stockton had already exhibited a flair for publicity that the navy was to find very useful in its unending task of squeezing appropriations out of Congress. He was a society figure in his own right, and he and John Tyler were close personal friends.

Dolley Madison would be among those present. That was taken for granted. The widow of the fourth President, a woman of Amazonian proportions, at seventy-something was the acknowledged social arbiter of Washington. She lived right across the street from the White House, and she knew everybody and everybody knew and loved her.

There would also be Senator Thomas Hart Benton, the bombastical Missourian, Abel Upshur, the new Secretary of State, Thomas W. Gilmer, the Secretary of the Navy, Captain Beverley Kennon, chief of the Navy Bureau of Construction, and many others.

They cast off a little before noon, a gay throng gaily

dressed, chatty, in high spirits, and at Alexandria they took on a band of musicians, who thereafter played indefatigably. It was a beautiful bright, chilly day, not a cloud in the sky. Along the shore stubborn masses of ice were breaking off, giving themselves over to the current, turning around and around lazily as they drifted downstream.

The skipper's somewhat startling nickname, "Fighting Bob," had been bestowed upon him as a young lieutenant in Mediterranean waters when he showed a propensity for getting into duels with junior officers of the Royal Navy. In fact he was anything but a belligerent man. Here, among these brilliant guests—there were about four hundred of them—he was at his best, the genial host who was everywhere. Most graciously, again and again, did he point out the wonders of this, the pride of the United States Navy, and especially the Oregon and the Peacemaker.

Despite the changeover from wood to iron, sail to steam, the broadside was still the navy's chief weapon. Boarding was too uncertain, chasing too chancy. The way to win a fight at sea was to get up close to the enemy and pound him to pieces with solid shot, in one volley or two. A warship it might have taken years to build could be sunk with all hands in minutes. The *Princeton* mounted twenty-four 42-pound carronades for this purpose. The weapon, a sort of seagoing mortar, had been called by its inventor, Robert Melville, a "smasher." It was *officially* designated the carronade by the Royal Navy when it was adopted by that service, after the Carron ironworks on the Carron River in Stirlingshire, Scotland. The *Princeton* also mounted, forward, two long guns for chasing purposes, and these Captain Stockton had christened Peacemaker and Oregon.

They were the biggest naval guns in the world, and each could throw a 212-pound projectile a distance of more than three miles—defensively, of course. They were not twins. The Peacemaker, weighting almost ten tons, carried a fifteen-foot barrel, being the larger by a hair.

After the rich and influential guests had been coached in leaving their mouths open and stopping their ears with their forefingers against the terrific concussion of air, each of these long guns was fired time after time in the course of this jolly cruise down the river. The target was always an ice floe, the distance, the captain estimated, being all of three miles. The splash, each time, was clearly visible, and the islet of ice had disappeared. These guns, "Fighting Bob" assured his guests, could have dropped a ball smacketty-dab into a wastebasket even at that distance, if it had been possible to position such a basket on one of the floes.

The firing ceased at last. The navy's pride swung in a majestic half-circle and started back upriver; and the guests went below to get something to eat. There was a great deal of this, for "Fighting Bob" was not a man to do things by halves, and the champagne flowed like water.

As four o'clock approached, there came down word from the deck that Captain Stockton had granted the request of certain passengers up there that one of the long guns be fired again. Among these passengers, the men greatly outnumbered the women, and many of the men had gone above, leaving the festive cabin to the ladies and the socially inclined. Among the latter was John Tyler, who had agreed to go topside for the final shot, but who paused at the foot of the ladder. State Senator Gardiner of New York, to whom the President was being particularly pleasant, was above, but Gardiner's two attractive daughters, Julia and Margaret, to whom the President was being even *more* pleasant, were still in the cabin. They were making a fuss over John Tyler, which he liked.

Mrs. John Tyler, the dim Letitia, had died recently after a very long illness.

Nevertheless, he would have turned away and climbed to the deck had not somebody at just this moment thrust into his hand yet another glass of wine, announcing as he did so that there was to be another toast, a toast the President surely would not want to miss. Tyler smiled and turned and raised the glass.

That was when it happened.

There was a terrible noise, which was followed by an even more terrible silence. Nothing punctuated that silence, which seemed to last forever, a timeless void. There was no patter of small falling objects on the deck above. There were no groans, not even a whimper.

John Tyler and the other men rushed topside.

If there had been a newspaper reporter among them, he would inevitably have described the deck as a shambles, and he would have been right. The word, which originally meant a butcher's slaughtering place, has come to mean little more than a disorderly mess. But here abroad the *Princeton* there was truly—there was literally—a shambles. Bits of flesh, bloodied handfuls of hair were strewn on the deck, where there lay twisted bodies, some squirming, most of them still. The Secretary of State, Captain Kennon, Senator Benton, the Secretary of the Navy, John Tyler's own Negro valet Henry—to whom only a few minutes earlier he had given permission to go up and watch the last firing of the Peacemaker—and any number of sailors lay prone, their mouths open, the eyes rolled up, blood crawling from their nostrils. Twenty feet of the bulwark had been ripped away. Over everything there hung the acrid odor of gunpowder.

As help arrived, a certain stir was noticed among the figures scattered across the deck, and here and there a moan arose. Stout Senator Benton had somehow survived, and so had Captain Stockton, though both were badly shaken. Two of the sailors were so torn as to be almost unrecognizable, and three others had been badly mauled. Both of the Cabinet members were unquestionably dead, as were the President's valet and State Senator Gardiner; also Virgil Maxey, also Samuel Phelps. No lady had been hurt, for they were all below. The musicians, too, though stationed on deck, were not injured—their post had been at the stern.

The *Princeton* returned to Alexandria, whence the injured were taken by ferry to Washington and its hospital—the dead, eight of them, to the White House, by order of the President.

These corpses, draped in the national flag, remained in the East Room all the next day, while thousands filed past. Then they were given a bang-up military funeral, all eight at once, and buried in the national cemetery as though they were heroes downed in battle.

A court of inquiry was in order, of course, and it was as well that a new Secretary of the Navy be named before this got to work. (They never did learn, for sure, what had caused the explosion.) Even more pressing—or so it seemed to John Tyler—was the State Department appointment. The special ambassadors from Texas were on their way; and although the Assistant Secretary of State, who was now Acting Secretary, was quite capable of conducting annexation negotiations, the tender feelings of the Lone Star legates must be considered, and nothing less than a full-time Cabinet member would be acceptable. The President was being batted about like a shuttlecock by the friends of the many eligible candidates—of both parties.

He escaped this only when he went to New York to get married.

12

★ ★ ★

The Lady with the Greyhound

Lion Gardiner must have been quite a man. We know very little about him, nothing at all about his personal appearance. It was no more than his duty to be doughty; but was he tall? thick in the shoulders? of glowering aspect? We do know that he came to America in 1635—fifteen years before the first Tyler reached these shores—as a military engineer employed by the Connecticut Company on a four-year contract at £100 per year to build a fort at the mouth of the Connecticut River, which fort was to be named Saybrook after Lords Saye and Brooke, sponsors of the company. He was a professional soldier, yet not of the aristocracy, and of his military record we know nothing except that he seemed to have spent much of his life in the Low Countries—Holland, Zeeland, Belgium—which even then were known as the Cockpit of Europe. Fort

Saybrook obviously was built to hold back the Dutch of New Amsterdam (New York) rather than the Indians, more or less harmless in those parts, and it may be that Lion Gardiner's acquaintance with the Dutch was a reason for this employment. He did, however, necessarily have some contact with the Indians, and he seems in particular to have liked and even admired the Montauks, whose side he took in the history he wrote of the Pequod War. Their chief, for "ten coates of trading cloth" sold him Manchonake Island (now Gardiner's Island), 3,300 exceedingly fertile acres in Block Island Sound between the eastern end of Long Island Sound and the open Atlantic. The family still owns this, and has a home there.*

Julia and Margaret Gardiner, sisters, were the seventh in direct line from Lion. The family had flourished, its nearness to New York giving it a chance to invest in real estate that proved profitable. Julia and the even more vivacious Margaret had been brought up in an atmosphere that would soon be called high society, although then it was only called high-toned. They had learned French, they had dabbled in art, doing watercolors, and had even

*Lion Gardiner called the place the Isle of Man, which may be a clue to his own birthplace, but it has always been Gardiner's Island in history. It was called Gardiner's Island, for example, by William Kidd, who on his return from the Indian Ocean skipped the usual entrance to his home town, New York, to poke into Long Island Sound from the east. It was at Gardiner's Island that he conferred with his lawyer, James Emmot, a respected vestryman of Trinity Church, here too that he was reunited with his wife Sarah, and here that he asked his friend John Gardiner, then head of the family, to store for a little while what was left of the fabled treasure he'd brought back—mostly bolts of silk and calico—before he surrendered himself to the authorities at Boston. This "treasure" was not buried. It was seized by the Crown only a few days later, and Kidd's widow never got any part of it, nor did Lawyer Emmot.

read a few books. They had traveled for almost a year in Europe, and had curtsied deep, lisping "Your Majesty" before Vicky. Julia, in addition, kept an Italian greyhound.

Back in America, the girls found New York too American. They had come to feel the need of being near a seat of power; and Washington—cosmopolitan Washington, the city of foreign visitors and foreign tastes—seemed a suitable romping ground for them. So their father (their mother Juliette being in poor health) took them to the capital for the Congressional session, which was the social season there.

These three rented and furnished a whole floor of one of the town's most elegant boardinghouses, and they made a considerable splash in high circles. Both girls were pretty, the dad fittingly self-effacing. It was the custom to address him as "Senator," for he had served one term as a member of the New York State Senate, less because of any interest in Whig politics than because he seemed to think that he owed it to his family position to have some such title. In Washington, where most Senators were *national* Senators, this caused no confusion, though some found it amusing.

The girls were a considerable success in the capital, which Charles Dickens recently had called "a city of magnificent intentions." They went everywhere, met everybody, saw everything, and they received many proposals of marriage, which until the arrival of John Tyler on the scene they waved away.

The last time the fair Letitia had been seen downstairs at the Executive Mansion was January 31, 1842, when her daughter Elizabeth was married to William Waller. It is not likely, then, that Julia Gardiner ever met her, for Julia had not yet come to Washington at that time. The President had no difficulty in the matter of social management, Elizabeth doing the honors very efficiently until her marriage, after which a charming daughter-in-law, who came from a theatrical family, took over, but it was no secret that he would have welcomed a second wife. Margaret Gardiner, wittier than her sister and almost as lovely, seems never to have been considered. He was Julia's, from the first time they met.

Washington talked, of course, although there was never a hint of scandal. But Washington scarcely noticed when the President slipped away in the summer of '44, though it was known that the Gardiner girls were both in New York at the time.

New York itself seems scarcely to have noticed it. The President was no traveler. This was odd, for he loved to meet people, and he was still pushing for readmittance into the Democratic party. His one trip north while occupying the Executive Mansion on Pennsylvania Avenue had been a notable success. In June of '44, however, he had some reason to court obscurity.

They were married the morning of Wednesday, June 26, at the Church of the Ascension, Tenth Street and Fifth Avenue, by Bishop Onderdonk of the Protestant Episcopal see of New York, which then included Long Island and hence Gardiner's Island. The bride, who stood 5 feet 2—the President was a shade over 6 feet—had her black hair parted in the middle, with buns over the ears, and wore a simple white dress of lisse, with a gauze veil hanging from a circle of white flowers, and no jewelry. She was twenty-three, he fifty-four. Her mother, Juliette, who herself was nine years younger than the bridegroom, was present, as were Margaret and several brothers.

There were no reporters. The Polly Bodine murder trial occupied most of the front pages the next day, the ceremony at the Church of the Ascension being barely mentioned, and by the time the scribes came to realize what they had missed, Julia and John were already on their way to eastern Virginia, a honeymoon. Margaret went with them; but this caused no comment, for it was a custom of the time.

The White House was a mess. The President was paid his $25,000 a year salary in monthly installments, but he had no expense account, no sort of maintenance allowance. If chairs needed re-covering or a door called piteously for paint, the President either paid for the job out of his own pocket or else appealed to Congress—both houses—for a special appropriation. Congress was not inclined to grant any special appropriations to an "accidental" Chief Executive who had no party behind him, and John Tyler himself, who had been entertaining conscientiously, was in debt. Lion Gardiner's great-great-great-great-granddaughter, appalled by what she saw, did the best she could, although she had no loose money of her own. She turned out to be a good housekeeper, and as a hostess she was, as she'd meant to be, brilliant.

A Gardiner girl was not, in herself, a novelty in Washington. After all, Julia and Margaret had been "out" there for two seasons. But a First Lady of the Land who could run up and down stairs, who could start the dancing in the ballroom, was.

Tyler's three sons liked the bride right away, but of his four daughters—the Tylers always had big families, the President himself having been the sixth of eight children—two, Letitia and the youngest, Alice, didn't. There were no scenes, however.

Society, abashed, wanted a little more time to study the queen. Julia saw that they got this. "The lovely lady Presidentess," as the local papers always called her, entertained as assiduously as ever her hubby had, and every night, just at first, and most afternoons as well, there was something going on at the White House. The President himself, who habitually got up at dawn or before dawn, so arranged his work that, except in emergencies, he was free at night. He did this not only in order to please his darling wife but also, and perhaps chiefly, because he took his social duties more seriously. After all, his mother had been an Armistead—of the Tidewater Armisteads.

Once as a young Representative, John Tyler had seen the polka danced at the White House, and hadn't liked it. He described it in a letter to one of his daughters back in Williamsburg, thirteen years old at the time, as "a dance which you have never seen and which I do not desire to see you dance. It is rather vulgar, I think." Yet when Julia did the polka, it was fine. His Accidency had grown a lot younger since his Congress days.

Julia even introduced the waltz into the White House and was not condemned as "fast." She had a way about her.

At first the Tylers entertained every day, but soon they cut this down to evening parties on Thursdays and Saturdays (also of course on special occasions), receptions to anybody who could be called a distinguished visitor, a large levee once a month, and the customary all-day open house January 1 and July 4.

The mansion deteriorated materially, but its spirit soared. Just after the marriage, President Tyler's "corporal's guard" in Congress brought in a $20,000 appropriation bill for White House furnishings, but this was quashed. It got so that Julia's social secretary, a former New York *Herald* reporter, F. W. Thomas, called the White House "a disgrace—a contemptible disgrace to the nation," adding "Many of the chairs in the East Room would be kicked out of a brothel." Still, those who did not like John Tyler shook their heads and clucked their disapproving tongues over the pretentious goings-on at what they liked to call Tuileries on the Potomac.

These mutterers at least were denied an excuse to grumble about "petticoat government," for Julia, although she had trained herself to seem to take an intelligent interest in talk of high politics, in fact carefully refrained from expressing any opinions in this field. She remained, determinedly, what she had been during her debutante seasons in the capital—beautiful, flirtatious, and empty-headed. This, being in the southern-belle tradition, pleased the President. The mutterers, therefore, were obliged to concentrate upon the airs she gave herself as First Lady.

The Italian greyhound had been bad enough, but when she sallied forth to do her shopping and make her calls in a coach-*and-four,* it seemed to some downright showy. The four were spanking smart white beasts, too, "finer horses," remarked Senator Benton's youngest daughter Jessie—she who was married to ambitious young Frémont, the "Pathfinder"—"than those of the Russian minister." The Russian representative himself, however, made no remonstrance.

Even more shocking was the way she received, on formal occasions. She was invariably seated, usually in something long and white and bright, with a train, and always with some manner of headdress that suggested a tiara without ever claiming to be one. Rowed behind her, standing, were sometimes six, occasionally eight lovely and attentive young women in white, who did nothing else *but* stand there. "The vestal virgins" Washington called them.

Despite firm efforts by many, and despite her previous reputation for fashionable flirting—the over-the-fan type of flirting—there never was a scrap of scandal about the second Mrs. John Tyler. Indeed, it was often remarked how openly she loved her husband, seeming almost unable to keep her hands off him. "You spend *so much time* in kissing, things of more importance are left undone," her mother scolded her by letter from New York. And when the town's most fashionable daguerreotypist, one Phimb, did a dual portrait of them, there were many who thought the result shocking, these two stood so close together, practically *pawing* one another. (The picture, alas, like Phimb himself, has disappeared; and it can be assumed that some prudish executor removed it from among the assets of the Tyler estate, causing it to be destroyed.)

It must not be thought that with all these marital diversions the President neglected to pursue his specialty—foreign affairs. He kept the pressure on the Oregon negotiators, who were proving, quietly, persistently, that if left alone a little, they could come to a sound and satisfactory solution to that boundary problem, unaffected by bewhiskered pastors on horseback and shouts of "Fifty-four-forty or fight!" It was in Tyler's Administration that this knot was untied, although he got none of the credit for it. Caleb Cushing of Massachusetts, one of his most devoted followers, was sent forth with a suite of ten in the steam frigate *Missouri* to China, mysterious China, where on July 3, 1844, he signed the Treaty of Wang Hiya, giving the United States important trading privileges in that reluctantly accessible empire. Cushing had meant to go on to Japan, where under orders of the President he might have done the same thing again, but ill health forced his immediate return, and the Nipponese opening was left to Commodore Matthew Calbraith Perry in another warship, in another Administration, Fillmore's. Tyler's minister in Berlin, Henry Wheaton, coached from the White House, after many tries had come up with an advantageous trade agreement with the German *Zollverein* (customs union), something both France and Great Britain had been trying to do for years; but this was killed by the Senate of the 28th Congress, apparently for no other reason than that the honorable gentlemen could not bear to see His Accidency get credit for it.

Tyler had appointed Washington Irving our ambassador to Spain, John Howard Payne, the author of "Home Sweet Home," consul to Tunis, and had capped a long encouragement of Samuel F. B. Morse by sending the first message over the first commercial electric telegraph line, Washington to Baltimore.

These were good things. But when he named John C. Calhoun Secretary of State—that was the stupidest thing he ever did.

13

★ ★ ★

The Biggest Blast

John Caldwell Calhoun was infallible, though he alone was aware of this fact. A classical scholar, he was conversant with the ways in which the ancient Greeks had sought the truth, the ultimate answer. He knew about the oracles at Delphi, at Colchis, Dodona, Paphos, and he probably knew about haruspication too, though he would have passed this over as being too messy for a man of his position. But then, he needed no guidance from the past. He was his own oracle. His Pythoness was his intellect, which was the wonderment of all who encountered it. He had been educated at Yale, where he sometimes had occasion to correct the college president's ratiocination, and when he needed to know the answer to a knotty question, it was to his own inner self that he turned. Every answer that emerged was of course final. Whenever John C. Calhoun entered upon a new office—and he had been a federal officeholder all his adult life—it was with the decisiveness, the irrevocability, of a Moses coming down from Sinai with the Decalogue tablets tucked under his arm. When Calhoun spoke, there was nothing more to be said.

So, the man was insufferably self-righteous. He was starchy, he was pompous, a hurler of homemade thunderbolts. He always sounded as if he were speaking in capital letters. That victory-flushed Northerners found in him the villain of the piece when they examined the events that led up to the War Between the States, as the muttering Southerners found him the hero, a martyr, was because both of these after-the-fact finders took him at his own evaluation—something that nobody in his own day had done. John C. Calhoun was not a misunderstood statesman. He was not a statesman at all; he was a politician.*

He had voted for the preferential tariff when this first came before Congress, but when it was hoisted as a banner by the boss of the Whigs, the leading aspirant for the Presidency, Henry Clay—and especially when his pro-stand had failed to help him carry Pennsylvania in the pre-campaign jostling of 1824—Calhoun became aware of its danger to the South and fought it. He had, like Clay himself, been a War Hawk in 1810 and 1811, clamoring for a chance to conquer Canada and to annex Florida, but he sharply modified this stand when he saw that the War of 1812 only intensified the North's economic lead over his own section of the country. And now, with the extension of slavery an issue, he was again strongly in favor of Manifest Destiny—i.e., land grabbing. Moreover, he seemed to be growing Southerner and Southerner all the time.

*"A politician thinks of the next election, a statesman of the next generation." James Freeman Clark.

That John C. Calhoun honestly loved his native state need not be doubted, but it was not this love that led him along the road to secession. It was his ambition.

There was a saying in Congress that when Calhoun took snuff, all South Carolina sneezed. This was wrong, for two reasons. Calhoun did not take snuff. Neither did he smoke tobacco, and he touched liquor not at all and wine only on ceremonial occasions, wetting his lips at a toast. It is doubtful if he even swore. He did not seem human.† "The cast-iron man," Harriette Martineau found him.

What is more, "all South Carolina" in the case of John C. Calhoun did not mean what it would mean with another officeholder. South Carolina had the most exclusive, the least democratic suffrage laws of any state in the Union, and "all South Carolina" was in fact a mere handful of rich men—planters and Charleston merchants. That John C. Calhoun was a member of this clique was no accident. He had not inherited his acres at Fort Hill, his slaves, much less earned them—he had married them. Moreover, he did not have too firm a grip on his fellow firebrands, and his influence elsewhere was negligible. He was a sectionalist not by choice but by necessity. Not until after the so-called Inevitable Conflict did the myth of his infallibil-

†"Jefferson prowling among the brickmasons at the University, Jackson with his clay pipe on the veranda of the Hermitage, Webster among the cattle at Marshfield, Clay meditating speeches under the trees at Ashland, are possible of contact by future generations, but Calhoun at Fort Hill seems hopelessly remote and cannot be visualized. He stalks upon the stage, a dramatic and impressive figure, and plays his public part, but no one is admitted to the dressing-room." Bowers, *Party Battles,* pp. 254–55. "Calhoun was a tiresome person. One wearies of his dry, humorless, logical writings as of the Noble Roman pose of his portraits, hand resting on heart, handsome features, and glaring eyes. But we must admit his intelligence and his sincerity." Morison, *Oxford History,* p. 432.

ity emerge, chrysalislike, from its quivering cocoon. Those who worked with him in Washington were in awe of his intellect, but they knew him, principally, as a man who wanted to become President.

He might have made a good President. He had served, competently, as a United States Senator, as Secretary of War, as Vice President. He could get things done. He was not so high-minded that he had forgotten how to work.

The Secretaryship of State was, indeed, the one high office, this side of the White House itself, that he never had occupied.

But—why *did* Tyler appoint him? This has puzzled historians. Surely the President was not unaware of Calhoun's egotism. "The great 'I am,' " he called him privately. Surely he knew the man's aversion to second place.

The easy explanation is that offered by a Congressman from Virginia, Henry A. Wise, who in his *Seven Decades* tells us that he himself had suggested the appointment to Calhoun, through a mutual friend, in such a way that Calhoun would think that it came from the President himself, thus trapping Mr. Tyler into fulfilling a promise he had never made. This information Congressman Wise imparted to the President—they were close friends—a few days later at breakfast. The President blew up, but when he had finished cursing, he muttered a begrudging assent. The President's own son and secretary, John Jr., backs this story, which nevertheless must be doubted. In the first place, politicians, like actors, when they write their memoirs, make unreliable witnesses. It is not that they are habitual liars, though many are; it is because they tend to dramatize everything, with themselves in the central role. In the second place, why should John Tyler accede to such an agreement, made behind his back, with a power-hungry rival? Calhoun would unquestionably grace the office, and he was strong for the annexation of Texas, but he was another Southerner in a Cabinet that now consisted almost entirely of Southerners, and he was inextricably linked to the cause of slavery extension.

No matter. Tyler named him, pointing out as he did so that the Texas situation, like that of Oregon, needed an expert hand, and Calhoun, with elephantine gestures of reluctance, accepted: "Nothing short of the magnitude of the crisis occasioned by the pending negotiations, could induce me to leave my retirement," he wrote to the President, and then he skedaddled back to Washington.

The President must have done this because he thought it might help him to be readmitted to the Democratic party, where his heart had always been. Nobody else thought that in early 1844 he stood the smallest chance of election to the Presidency, but hope springs eternal in the human breast, and John Tyler's was an especially virulent case of Potomac fever.

Almost immediately the new Secretary of State embarrassed his boss by reading a sermon to Lord Aberdeen, the genial Scot who had taken Lord Palmerston's place at the Foreign Office.

Great Britain recently (1833) had freed all of the slaves in her West Indian empire, paying the owners a compensation of about $100 million. Now she was engaged in trying to stamp out the trans-Atlantic slave traffic, and she appealed to the United States to help in this effort. Tyler already had turned down a similar appeal, coldly but politely, for he was himself a slave owner and a believer in the Peculiar Institution, although he did everything possible to avoid the subject in public because of its dangerous divisiveness. Calhoun, however, appealed to, broke forth in a tirade against abolition, pointing out to the astonished peer that slavery was not only sanctioned by the Bible and by all right-thinking men everywhere, but was absolutely necessary for the continued well-being of the human race. Calhoun could do this sort of thing in a manner most pontifical, saying the final word on the matter, silencing all others. Aberdeen must have blinked for a moment when he read the message; but he simply dropped the subject.

John Tyler at least had established the *re*annexation of Texas as the main issue of the coming, the 1844, campaign. Both of the leading preconvention candidates, Martin Van Buren for the Democrats, Henry Clay for the Whigs, had come out with statements—issued simultaneously, by prearrangement, April 27, 1844—tut-tutting this issue with the greatest of care. The time, both said timorously, was not yet ripe. Clay thereupon lost any chance he might have had of carrying a single Southern state, whereas Van Buren in effect was shouted down. "You might as well try to turn the current of the Mississippi River as to try to turn the Democrats against annexation," declared the Old Hero, Andrew Jackson, from his retirement; and it seemed as though he were right.

Henry Clay had his Whig party well in hand, and he was nominated without trouble. Van Buren's case was different. When the Democrats assembled May 27 at the Odd Fellows Hall, North Gay Street, Baltimore, they were still using the two-thirds rule they had adopted in 1832 to renominate Jackson, used again in '35 for Martin Van Buren, dropped in '39, and taken up again in '43 (after which it remained in force until 1936), despite the fact that their opponents, first the Whigs, then the Republicans, always had majority-vote nominations. This was too much for Van Buren, who had been far ahead at first but lost ground jerkily until the ninth ballot, when a Tennessean, James Knox Polk, came up from behind to snatch the prize.

Polk was the nation's first "dark horse." He had been in public life for many years, had been governor of Tennessee, speaker of the national House of Representatives, and, like Van Buren, was known as an Andrew Jackson protégé. When Van Buren was elected President in 1835, it was murmured that Old Hickory had been succeeded by Slippery Elm. When Polk was nominated, he was often called what a brother of Herman Melville the novelist had called him, Little Hickory. He was no knight in shining armor, no gallant champion. He was short and skinny, with an outjutting law, thin lips, a face that had never been disfigured by a smile. He had a highly uningratiating manner. Tense, tireless, he ran a tight ship, as seamen would say, and was constantly scowling over his assistants' shoulders.

The Democratic party platform, adopted at this same convention, called for "the *re*annexation of Texas and the *re*occupation of Oregon."

The issue, then, would be put before the people.

This boost came barely in time. The cause of *re*annexation had been seen to sag piteously, and John C. Calhoun, for all his faith in himself, had shaken a discouraged head until his chief upbraided him—him!—and went so far as to threaten to dismiss him if he didn't work harder in this cause. But now it was a national issue, all John Tyler had ever asked.

Unexpectedly too at this time a couple of states, New

England, New Hampshire and Maine, adopted resolutions in favor of accepting Texas into the Union.

Tyler's friends staged an independent national convention for him in Baltimore, the walls being hung with "TYLER AND TEXAS!" banners, but he never really tried to start a third party, and after a while, with the Clay-Polk contest looming close, in a letter to Andrew Jackson he specifically withdrew his name. He stipulated only that the friends who had stuck to him, the friends he had appointed to office, be retained. General Jackson's letter of thanks for this action was taken by some to be a formal readmittance of John Tyler into the Democratic party, but James K. Polk and his advisers did not accept it, and when the changeover came, no mercy was shown to the Tyler appointees.

Polk won the '44 election. The unexpectedly strong showing of the new Liberty party, the abolitionists' party, blocked him from a majority; but his plurality was substantial.

Still the Senate, a lame-duck body now, kept saying no to Texas. Since the razzle-dazzle of the Log Cabin and Hard Cider campaign, the alignment in Congress had been changed. Clay no longer ruled the roost on *both* sides of the big white dome. As a result of the '42 election, the Whig majority of 25 in the House had become a Democratic majority of 60, but the crusty old Senate still could not muster a two-thirds confirmation of any *re*annexation treaty.

Then Calhoun's son-in-law came to the rescue with a startling snippet of information from London. Duff Green, a newspaperman, was in the mother country as a sort of unofficial observer, or spy, for the Secretary of State. He reported, excitedly, that Lord Aberdeen's Foreign Office was flirting with the Republic of Texas, and it was a flirtation that might lead to marriage. In other words, Texas could at any time become a British protectorate. England would pay off the new nation's huge debt, guarantee her boundaries, lend money against her public lands, buy all the cotton she could produce, *and* record her solemn renunciation of slavery.

Duff Green's informants had been mistaken as to the actual details of this oglement, but that it was a fact cannot now be doubted. Soon came confirmation from W. S. Murphy, the United States chargé in Texas, and his able successor, Andrew Jackson Donelson, who both reported that Sam Houston, president of Texas again, was clearly coming to the opinion that it would be better to continue as head of his own republic than to become simply another governor or Senator. Indeed Houston himself was later to admit—and more than once, when in his cups—that he had "coquetted a bit" with Great Britain. He, however, was to say nothing about France, which was also believed to have designs on the Lone Star Republic.

The advantages to both sides of an Anglo-Texan understanding were obvious. Texas could gain economic freedom and be relieved of her fear of Mexico, which still had not recognized the Texan government and might at any time that her politics permitted beat the strayed lamb back into the fold. Great Britain, which already had a firm base to the north of the United States, would then have a base to the south as well, effectively blocking the Yankee advance upon California. Britain too would be in a position to pinch off the mouth of the Mississippi, which had become the lifeline of the United States—in the event, considered likely by many on both sides, of another war between these two. The American monopoly of cotton production—for it amounted to that—would be broken. The spread of slavery would be stopped, which would mean slavery's death by slow strangulation.

Lord Aberdeen, always helpful, at this critical juncture came up with a suggestion. If the annexation of Texas was rejected by the U.S. Senate, as seemed likely, Aberdeen proposed what he called a "diplomatic act," a sort of perpetual treaty, to be subscribed to by Britain, France, Texas, Mexico, and the United States. Texas should agree not to increase her boundaries and never to be joined to the United States. Everybody would guarantee everybody else's sovereignty. If Mexico balked, she should be forced in by the simple process of twisting her arm, though Lord Aberdeen did not put it that way.

The France of Louis Philippe was said to have been interested in this "diplomatic act" just at first, but she soon became suspicious of Britain's motives and withdrew from the negotiations.

Tyler, of course, would have no part of it.

The barrel-chested Thomas Hart Benton, in a Senate speech of two hours—laconic for him—had stigmatized the effort to annex Texas as "a base, wicked, miserable, presidential intrigue," and this is the way the diehards thought of it. To them it was a brash bid for personal popularity, nothing more, and there was even another impeachment movement started, the charge being that the President had exceeded his authority. But now, with the introduction of English competition into the issue, this was changed. The envoys from Washington-on-the-Brazos suddenly found the road to Union much smoother. The United States would accept Texas directly, without the need for going through a stage of territorial status, as previously proposed. The United States would agree that the new state could break itself into as many as four states, if it wished, without asking the permission of the federal government. The United States would not take over the newcomer's debt, as the original federal government, thanks to the first Secretary of the Treasury, Alexander Hamilton, had taken over the debts of the original thirteen states, but the United States would buy up the Texas public lands at a mighty handsome price. Even then the Texas negotiators in Washington-on-the-Potomac wavered. They had their instructions. They must demand, again, that the United States should take steps by land and by sea to block any invasion of Lone Star territory by the Republic of Mexico while negotiations were in progress. The chargé on the Brazos, Murphy at that time, already had promised such troop and warship movements, but President Tyler had disclaimed this promise, which had been made without his knowledge. Now, however, John Tyler informally but firmly ordered several regiments to the Texas–Louisiana line, while his friend Commodore Stockton, acting under equally informal orders, off the record, led a small fleet to the western reaches of the Gulf of Mexico. This *could* touch off a war with Mexico, edgy as a race horse, but Tyler didn't think it would.

Still those mossbacks in the Senate held out against annexation. John Tyler consulted his Secretary of State yet again, and they decided to take a leaf from Lord Aberdeen's book and get themselves a treaty by simply calling it something else. A joint resolution, originating at the White House, would not call for a two-thirds Senate confirmation, only for a majority vote in each house. So they framed a joint resolution; and it was passed.

This was done barely in time. Signing it, March 2, 1845,

was the last official act of John Tyler as President. He sent it off to Texas immediately, that very night, instead of holding it open for the incoming executive, Mr. Polk, for he wished to make sure that his Administration got the credit.

Socially that Administration went out with a splash. Its biggest blast at the White House was its last, Wednesday, February 18. Two thousand were invited, three thousand came. In an expression that was current, the party was "squeezy." Yet nobody fainted, nobody got into a fight, and indeed they all seemed to have a good time, while Julia, the "lovely lady Presidentess," flanked by her vestal virgins, beamed upon them. The red-coated Marine band played pauselessly. The punch bowls were refilled again and again, and though some attempt was made to limit it to the important guests, champagne in the amount of eight cases was consumed. There were more than six hundred candles, frequently changed, in the four rooms. The candles alone, it was reported, had cost $350.

It was the grandest high-toned entertainment that Washington ever had witnessed.

"Well," said a bemused John Tyler, when the last guest had hiccupped his way out and servants were beginning to clean up, "now at least they can't say that I have been a President without a party."

14

★ ★ ★

The Last of the Line

I strove with one, for none was worth my strife.
Nature I loved, and, after Nature, Art:
I warm'd both hands before the fire of life;
It sinks, and I am ready to depart.

—Walter Savage Landor

The barge was called *Pocahontas*, it is not clear why. The daughter of the chief of the Powhatans was a Virginian, to be sure, and as Mrs. John Rolfe she was distinctly an FFV. (First Families of Virginia), but she had no connection with Sherwood Forest, the sixteen-hundred-acre estate the President had purchased for $1,200—just before his marriage to Julia Gardiner. It was on the north bank of the James, about twenty-seven miles southeast of Richmond, and they were building a mansion there. Why Sherwood Forest? The ex-President would smile at the question. "Because it's a good place for an outlaw," he would reply. But nobody ever did know why the barge was called *Pocahontas*.

It had been decorated by Julia herself, and was predominantly blue. It had cushions of damask satin trimmed with blue, and the four oarsmen, all black—there were about sixty slaves at Sherwood Forest—wore white pants and blue-checked calico shirts. They had patent-leather belts, very smart, and their hats were painted blue with "Pocahontas" in white. In one corner of their shirt collars was worked in braid a bow-and-arrow, in the other Julia's and Tyler's initials intertwined.

Did he sometimes wonder, the ex-President, as he was wafted across the waters toward the south shore, where they often picnicked, did he wonder what it would have been like if William Henry Harrison had not caught that killing cold right after his inauguration? For the land over there, unused just now, was Harrison land. The Tidewater Harrisons. The family the old general had belonged to.

The James is not wide, but it must occasionally have seemed a very long distance from Tyler on the north bank to Tippecanoe on the south. It must have seemed as if all the world were between.

He was no fire-eater, though he had once given a speech before the Virginia legislature so bellicose that it caused the editor of the Richmond *Examiner* to echo Lady Macbeth: "Yet who would have thought the old man to have had so much blood in him?" Ordinarily his voice was raised only in favor of moderation, and after his return from the White House, he declined all offers of public posts unless they promised a hope of keeping his state in the Union. He did accept the chairmanship of the Peace Conference, a last-minute effort to hold the states together. In this capacity he personally pleaded with James ("Old Buck") Buchanan, the fourteenth President of the United States, who was about to turn over his office to the newly elected Abraham Lincoln. But since he could speak only for Virginia and not for all the states of the South, some of which had already seceded, this plea fell flat.

He might have remained there in Washington when the final break did come—he was assured of an honorable place in the federal government. But of course he returned to Virginia, as his duty dictated.

He did agree to be elected to the Confederate House of Representatives, although he declined to stand for the Senate, which carried a six-year term, on the ground that he probably wouldn't last that long. He was right. He died, quietly, January 18, 1862, the last of the Virginia Dynasty, already a forgotten man.

Bibliography

Adams, Ephraim Douglass. *British Interests and Activities in Texas, 1838–1846*. Baltimore: The Johns Hopkins Press, 1910.

Adams, John Quincy. *Memoirs of John Quincy Adams*, ed. Charles Francis Adams. 12 volumes. Philadelphia: J. B. Lippincott & Co., 1874–77.

Alexander, DeAlva Stanwood. *A Political History of the State of New York*. 3 volumes. New York: Henry Holt and Company, 1909.

Alexander, Holmes. *The American Talleyrand: The Career and Contemporaries of Martin Van Buren, Eighth President*. New York: Russell & Russell, 1968.

Bancroft, Frederic. *Calhoun and the South Carolina Nullification Movement*. Baltimore: The Johns Hopkins Press, 1928.

———*The Life of William H. Seward*. 2 volumes. New York: Harper and Brothers Publishers, 1900.

Bancroft, Hubert Howe. *History of the North Mexican States and Texas*. San Francisco: A. L. Bancroft & Company, 1889.

Barker, Eugene C. "The Influence of Slavery in the Colonization of Texas," *Mississippi Valley Historical Review*. Vol. XI, no. 1, June 1924, pp. 85–98.

———*The Life of Stephen F. Austin, Founder of Texas, 1793–1836*. Nashville and Dallas: The Cokesbury Press, 1926.

———"President Jackson and the Texas Revolution," *American Historical Review*. Vol. XII, p. 788.

Bassett, John Spencer. *The Life of Andrew Jackson*. New York: The Macmillan Company, 1928.

Bemis, Samuel Flagg. *A Diplomatic History of the United States*. New York: Henry Holt and Company, Inc., 1928.

———*The Latin American Policy of the United States: An Historical Interpretation*. New York: Harcourt, Brace and Company, 1943.

Benton, Thomas Hart. *Thirty Years View: or, A History of the Working of the American Government for Thirty Years, from 1820 to 1850*. 2 volumes. New York: D. Appleton Company, 1854.

Binkley, William Campbell. *The Expansionist Movement in Texas, 1846–1848*. Berkeley: University of California Press, 1925.

———*The Texas Revolution*. Baton Rouge: Louisiana State University Press, 1952.

———, ed. *Official Correspondence of the Texas Revolution, 1835–1836*. 2 volumes. New York: D. Appleton-Century Company, 1936.

Boucher, Chauncey Samuel. "The Annexation of Texas and the Bluffton Movement in South Carolina," *Mississippi Valley Historical Review*. Vol. VI, no. 1, June 1919.

———*The Nullification Controversy in South Carolina*. Chicago: University of Chicago Press, 1916.

Bowers, Claude G. *The Party Battles of the Jackson Period*. Boston: Houghton Mifflin Company, 1922.

Bradford, Gamaliel. *As God Made Them*. Boston: Houghton Mifflin Co., 1929.

Buell, Augustus C. *History of Andrew Jackson: Pioneer, Soldier, Politician, President*. 2 volumes. New York: Charles Scribner's Sons, 1904.

Burgess, John W. *The Middle Period, 1817–1858*. New York: Charles Scribner's Sons, 1924.

Callahan, James Morton. *American Foreign Policy in Mexican Relations*. New York: The Macmillan Company, 1932.

Callcott, Wilfred Hardy. *Santa-Anna: The Story of an Engigma Who Once Was Mexico*. Norman: University of Oklahoma Press, 1936.

Capers, Gerald M. *John C. Calhoun, a Reappraisal*. Gainesville, Fla. University of Florida Press, 1960.

Carroll, E. Malcolm. *Origins of the Whig Party*. Gloucester, Mass.: Peter Smith, 1964.

Castaneda, Carlos E., ed. *The Mexican Side of the Texas Revolution*. Austin and Dallas: Graphic Ideas, Incorporated, 1970.

Catterall, Ralph C. H. *The Second Bank of the United States*. Chicago: Chicago University Press, 1903.

Cave, Alfred A. *Jacksonian Democracy and the Histo-*

rians. Gainesville, Fla. The University of Florida Press, 1964.

Chitwood, Oliver Perry. *John Tyler: Champion of the Old South*. New York: D. Appleton-Century Company, 1939.

Cleaves, Freeman. *Old Tippecanoe: William Henry Harrison and His Time*. New York: Charles Scribner's Sons, 1939.

Coit, Margaret L. *John C. Calhoun: American Portrait*. Boston: Houghton Mifflin Company, 1950.

Cole, Arthur Charles. *The Whig Party in the South*. Washington: Oxford University Press, 1913.

Corey, Albert B. *The Crisis of 1830–1842 in Canadian-American Relations*. New Haven: Yale University Press, 1941.

Current, Richard N. *Daniel Webster and the Rise of National Conservatism*. Boston: Little, Brown and Company, 1955.

Curtis, James C. *The Fox at Bay: Martin Van Buren and the Presidency, 1837–1841*. Lexington: University of Kentucky Press, 1970.

Dangerfield, George. *The Era of Good Feelings*. New York: Harcourt, Brace & Co., 1952.

Dinnerstein, Leonard. "The Accession of John Tyler to the Presidency," *Virginia Magazine of History and Biography*. October 1962, pp. 447–458.

Eaton, Clement. *Henry Clay and the Art of American Politics*. Boston: Little, Brown and Company, 1957.

Fish, Carl Russell. *The Civil Service and the Patronage*. Cambridge: Harvard University Press, 1920.

———*The Rise of the Common Man, 1830–1850.* New York: The Macmillan Company, 1927.

Foote, Henry Stuart. *Texas and the Texans.* 2 volumes. Philadelphia: Thomas & Company, 1841.

Fox, Dixon Ryan. *The Decline of Aristocracy in the Politics of New York.* New York: Columbia University Press, 1919.

Fraser, Hugh Russell. *Democracy in the Making: The Jackson-Tyler Era.* Indianapolis: The Bobbs-Merrill Company, 1938.

Fuess, Claude Moore. *Daniel Webster.* Boston: Little, Brown and Company, 1930.

Gambrell, Herbert. *Anson Jones, the Last President of Texas.* Garden City, N.Y.: Doubleday & Company, Inc., 1948.

Gammon, Samuel Rhea. *The President Campaign of 1832. Baltimore: The Johns Hopkins Press, 1922.*

Garrison, George Pierce. "The First Stage of the Movement for the Annexation of Texas," *American Historical Review.* Vol. X, 72–96.

———*Westward Extension, 1841–1850.* New York: Harper & Brothers Publishers, 1906.

Gatell, Frank Otto, and John M. McFall, ed. *Jacksonian America, 1815–1840; New Society, Changing Politics.* Englewood Cliffs, N.J.: Prentice-Hall, Inc., 1970.

Graebner, Norman A. "James K. Polk: A Study in Federal Patronage," *Mississippi Valley Historical Review.* Vol. XXXVIII, March 1952.

Greeley, Horace. *Recollections of a Busy Life.* New York: J. B. Ford & Co., 1869.

Green, Constance McLaughlin. *Washington, Capital*

City. 2 volumes. Princeton, N.J.: Princeton University Press, 1962–3.

Green, James A. *William Henry Harrison: His Life and Times*. Richmond, Va.: Garrett and Massie, Incorporated, 1941.

Gunderson, Robert Gray. *The Log-Cabin Campaign*. Lexington: The University of Kentucky Press, 1957.

Hall, Claude H. *Abel Parker Upshur, Conservative Virginian, 1790–1844*. Madison: State Historical Society of Wisconsin, 1964.

Hammond, Bray. *Banks and Politics in America, from the Revolution to the Civil War*. Princeton, N.J.: Princeton University Press, 1957.

Hammond, Jared Delano. *The History of Political Parties in the State of New York*. New York: H. & E. Phinney, 1846.

Herring, Pendleton. *The Politics of Democracy: American Parties in Action*. New York: W. W. Norton & Company, Inc., 1940.

Hofstadter, Richard. *The Idea of a Party System: The Rise of Legitimate Opposition in the United States, 1780–1840*. Berkeley and Los Angeles: University of California Press, 1969.

Hogan, William Ransom. *The Texas Republic: A Social and Economic History*. Norman: University of Oklahoma Press, 1946.

Hone, Philip. *The Diary of Philip Hone, 1828–1951*, Allan Nevins, ed. 2 volumes. New York: Dodd, Mead and Company, 1927.

Hudson, Frederic. *Journalism in the United States, from 1690 to 1872*. New York: Harper & Brothers, 1873.

Hugins, Walter. *Jacksonian Democracy and the Working Class*. Stanford, Calif: Stanford University Press, 1960.

Lambert, Oscar Doane. *Presidential Politics in the United States, 1841–1844*. Durham, N.C.: Duke University Press, 1936.

McCarthy, Charles. "The Antimasonic Party," *Annual Report of the American Historical Associations*. 1902, pp. 367–574.

McCormick, Richard P. *The Second American Party System: Party Formation in the Jacksonian Era*. Chapel Hill: University of North Carolina Press, 1966.

Martineau, Harriet. *Society in America*. 2 volumes. New York and London: Saunders & Otley, 1837.

Mayo, Bernard. *Henry Clay: Spokesman of the New West*. Boston: Houghton Mifflin Company, 1937.

Meigs, William M. *The Life of John Caldwell Calhoun*. 2 volumes. New York: G. E. Stechert & Co., 1917.

Merk, Frederick. *Manifest Destiny and Mission in American History: A Reinterpretation*. New York: Alfred A. Knopf, 1963.

———*The Monroe Doctrine and American Expansion, 1843–1849*. New York: Alfred A. Knopf, 1966.

———*The Oregon Question: Essays on Anglo-American Diplomacy and Politics*. Cambridge: Harvard University Press, 1971.

———"A Safety Valve Thesis and Texas Annexation," *Mississippi Valley Historical Review*. Vol. XLIX, no. 3, December 1962.

———*Slavery and the Annexation of Texas*. New York: Alfred A. Knopf, 1972.

———and Lois Bannister. *Fruits of Propaganda in the Tyler Administration.* Cambridge: Harvard University Press, 1967.

Merriam, Charles Edward, and Harold Foote Gosnell. *The American Party System: An Introduction to the Study of Political Parties in the United States.* New York: The Macmillan Company, 1949.

Meyers, Marvin. *The Jacksonian Persuasion: Politics and Belief.* Stanford, Calif: Stanford University Press, 1957.

Miller, Hunter. *Treaties and Other International Acts of the United States of America.* Volumes 1 through 5. Washington: Government Printing Office, 1931–1937.

Morgan, Robert J. *A Whig Embattled: The Presidency under John Tyler.* Lincoln: University of Nebraska Press, 1954.

Morison, Samuel Eliot. *Harrison Gray Otis, 1765–1848: The Urbane Federalist.* Boston: Houghton Mifflin Company, 1969.

———*The Oxford History of the American People.* New York: Oxford University Press, 1965.

Mowry, Arthur May. *The Dorr War, or The Constitutional Struggle in Rhode Island.* Providence, R. I.: Preston & Rounds Co., 1901.

Nathans, Sydney. *Daniel Webster and Jacksonian Democracy.* Baltimore: Johns Hopkins University Press, 1975.

Nichols, Roy F. *The Invention of the American Political Parties.* New York: The Macmillan Company, 1967.

Nixon, Oliver W. *How Marcus Whitman Saved Oregon.* Chicago: Star Publishing Company, 1895.

Norton, Anthony Banning. *Reminiscences of the Log Cabin and Hard Cider Campaign*, and *Tippecanoe Songs of the Log Cabin Boys and Girls of 1840*. Mount Vernon, Ohio, and Dallas, Texas: A. B. Norton & Co., 1888.

Parish, John Carl. *The Emergence of the Idea of Manifest Destiny*. Los Angeles: University of California Press, 1932.

Parton, James. *Life of Andrew Jackson*. 3 volumes. New York: Mason Brothers, 1861.

Pessen, Edward, *Jacksonian America: Society, Personality, and Politics*. Homewood, Ill.: The Dorsey Press, 1960.

——— *Most Uncommon Jacksonians: The Radical Leaders of the Early Labor Movements*. Albany: State University of New York Press, 1967.

Pletcher, David M. *The Diplomacy of Annexation: Texas, Oregon, and the Mexican War*. Columbia: University of Missouri Press, 1973.

Poage, George Rawlings. *Henry Clay and the Whig Party*. Chapel Hill: University of North Carolina Press, 1936.

Reeves, Jesse S. *American Diplomacy under Tyler and Polk*. Baltimore: The Johns Hopkins Press, 1907.

Remini, Robert V. *Martin Van Buren and the Making of the Democratic Party*. New York: Columbia University Press, 1959.

———, ed. *The Age of Jackson*. Columbia: University of South Carolina Press, 1972.

Rippey, J. Fred. "Diplomacy of the United States and Mexico regarding the Isthmus of Tehuantepec," *Mis-*

sissippi Valley Historical Review. Vol. VI, no. 4, March 1920.

———*The United States and Mexico*. New York: Alfred A. Knopf, 1926.

Rives, George Lockhart. *The United States and Mexico, 1821–1848*. 2 volumes. New York: Charles Scribner's Sons, 1913.

Roosevelt, Theodore. *Thomas Hart Benton*. New York: Charles Scribner's Sons, 1926.

Rozwene, Edwin C., ed. *Ideology and Power in the Age of Jackson*. New York: New York University Press, 1964.

Schlesinger, Arthur M., Jr. *The Age of Jackson*. Boston: Little, Brown and Company, 1945.

Schurz, Carl. *Henry Clay*. 2 volumes. Boston: Houghton Mifflin Company, 1899.

Seager, Robert, III. *And Tyler Too: A Biography of John & Julia Gardiner Tyler*. New York: McGraw-Hill Book Company, Inc., 1963.

Sellers, Charles Grier, Jr., ed. *Andrew Jackson, Nullification, and the State-Rights Tradition*. Chicago: Rand McNally & Company, 1963.

Sharp, James Roger. *The Jacksonians versus the Banks: Politics in the States after the Panic of 1837*. New York: Columbia University Press, 1970.

Shepard, Edward M. *Martin Van Buren*. Boston: Houghton, Mifflin and Company, 1890.

Shurtleff, Harold R. *The Log Cabin Myth: A Study of the Early Dwellings of English Colonists in North America*. Gloucester, Mass.: Peter Smith, 1967.

Slotkin, Richard. *Regeneration Through Violence: The Mythology of the American Frontier, 1600–1860*. Middletown, Conn.: Wesleyan University Press, 1973.

Smith, Justin. *The Annexation of Texas.* New York: Barnes & Noble, Inc., 1941.

Smith, Walter Buckinham. *Economic Aspects of the Second Bank of the United States.* Cambridge: Harvard University Press, 1953.

Sperber, Hans. " 'Fifty-four Forty or Fight': Facts and Fictions." *American Speech.* Vol. XXXII, no. 1, February 1957.

Stanwood, Edward. *A History of the Presidency from 1788 to 1897.* Boston: Houghton Mifflin Company, 1898.

Stephenson, Nathaniel W. *Texas and the Mexican War.* New Haven: Yale University Press, 1921.

Sumner, Charles Graham. *Protectionism.* New York: Henry Holt and Co., 1885.

Sumner, William Graham. *Andrew Jackson.* Boston: Houghton Mifflin Co., 1910.

Syrett, Harold G. *Andrew Jackson: His Contribution to the American Tradition.* Indianapolis: The Bobbs-Merrill Company, Inc., 1953.

Taussig, F. W. *The Tariff History of the United States.* New York: G. P. Putnam's Sons, 1914.

Temin, Peter. *The Jacksonian Economy.* New York: W. W. Norton & Co., 1969.

Turner, Frederick Jackson. *The Rise of the New West.* New York: Harper & Brothers Publishers, 1906.

———*The United States, 1830–1850: The Nation and Its Sections.* New York: Henry Holt and Company, 1935.

Tyler, Alice Felt. *Freedom's Ferment: Phases of American Social History to 1860.* Minneapolis: University of Minnesota Press, 1944.

Van Buren, Martin. *Autobiography*. Edited by John C. Fitzpatrick. New York: Augustus M. Kelley, 1969.

Van Deusen, Glyndon G. *The Jacksonian Era, 1828–1848*. New York: Harper and Row, Publishers, 1959.

———*Thurlow Weed: Wizard of the Lobby*. New York: DeCapo Press, 1969.

Von Holst, H. *John C. Calhoun*. Boston: Houghton Mifflin Company, 1899.

Ward, John William. *Andrew Jackson: Symbol for an Age*. New York: Oxford University Press, 1955.

Weed, Thurlow. *The Life of Thurlow Weed*. Boston: Houghton Mifflin Company, 1883.

Weinberg, Albert K. *Manifest Destiny: A Study of Nationalist Expansion in American History*. Baltimore: The Johns Hopkins Press, 1935.

Wellman, Paul I. *The House Divides: The Age of Jackson and Lincoln, from the War of 1812 to the Civil War*. Garden City, N.Y.: Doubleday & Company, Inc., 1966.

White, Leonard D. *The Jacksonians: A Study in Administrative History, 1829–1861*. New York: The Macmillan Company, 1954.

Wiltse, Charles M. *John C. Calhoun, Nationalist, 1782–1828*. Indianapolis: The Bobbs-Merrill Company, 1944.

———*John C. Calhoun, Nullifier, 1829–1839*. Indianapolis: The Bobbs-Merrill Company, 1949.

———*John C. Calhoun, Sectionalist, 1839–1850*. Indianapolis: The Bobbs-Merrill Company, 1951.

Wise, Henry A. *Seven Decades of the Union*. Philadelphia: J. B. Lippincott Company, 1871.

Yoakum, Henderson. *History of Texas, from its first settlement to its annexation by the United States in 1846*. 2 volumes. New York: Redfield, 1850.

Zwelling, Shomer S. *Expansion and Imperialism*. Chicago: Loyola University Press, 1970.

Index

DATE DUE

30 505 JOSTEN'S			

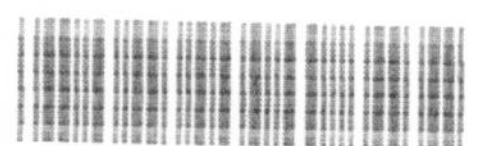